COZUMEL

COZUMEL

THE COMPLETE GUIDE

Patricia A. Holt

iUniverse, Inc.
New York Lincoln Shanghai

COZUMEL
THE COMPLETE GUIDE

iUniverse books may be ordered through booksellers or by contacting:

iUniverse
2021 Pine Lake Road, Suite 100
Lincoln, NE 68512
www.iuniverse.com
1-800-Authors (1-800-288-4677)

ISBN-13: 978-0-595-36995-9 (pbk)
ISBN-13: 978-0-595-81403-9 (ebk)
ISBN-10: 0-595-36995-2 (pbk)
ISBN-10: 0-595-81403-4 (ebk)

Printed in the United States of America

TABLE OF CONTENTS

INTRODUCTION ix

COZUMEL CALENDER xi

Chapter 1: GENERAL INFORMATION 1

The basics you need to know.

Chapter 2: GETTING THERE 7

Check out your options for travel.

Chapter 3: WHERE TO STAY 13

The many choices for lodging.

Chapter 4: GETTING AROUND COZUMEL 41

Auto-Bus-Taxi-Bike The choice is yours.

Chapter 5: DINING IN COZUMEL 49

From $2.00 to $100.00 +

Chapter 6: SHOP-SHOP-SHOP 83

Tee shirts to diamonds, you can find it on Cozumel.

Chapter 7: DIVING THE MAGICAL, MYSTICAL WATERS OF COZUMEL..93

An Underwater Magic Show

Chapter 8: FISHING FOR THE BIG ONE 121

Chapter 9: BEACHES-TOURS-THINGS TO DO 127

Impossible to get bored!

Chapter 10: MONEY-MEDICAL-CHURCHES-SPECIALTY SERVICES..139

All your needs can be met.

Chapter 11: COMMUNITY SERVICE 155

Open your heart and become a part of Cozumel.

Chapter 12: LET'S SPEAK SPANISH 163

Basic vacation Spanish.

Chapter 13: USEFUL INTERNET SITES 191

Includes discussion boards and lots of useful information.

A FEW FINAL TIPS BEFORE YOU GO 197

Dear Readers:

If you are reading this book, then I will assume that you are either planning or dreaming of a vacation in Cozumel. You will not regret this decision, I promise.

I have been visiting Cozumel for the past nine years and I can never get enough of it. Many people start planning a repeat visit even before they their first visit is over.

The one thing I have been unable to find over the past nine years is a comprehensive guide to Cozumel. None existed, until now! Yes I found a few books that would have one or two chapters pertaining to Cozumel, such as Frommer's, and an Idiots Guide to Mexico's Beaches, but nothing solely dedicated to this beautiful island.

I decided that I would solve this problem by writing a guide myself. This is the most complete guide you have ever read. You can travel on a shoe string or blow your bank account, the choice is yours. Which ever you decide, this book will be a welcome asset in planning your trip.

NOTE: As most are aware, Cozumel took a direct hit from Hurricane Wilma. I decided to go forward with this publication, as 85–95 percent of the business on the Isle will rebuild and be available to visitors. Do not believe all you read in the media, go to the discussion boards for the truth. Less than 1 week after the storm there were already hotels and dining available. I plan to put out an update in approximately 6 months. Cozumel needs your tourist dollars more than ever and they will work hard to deserve them.

INTRODUCTION TO COZUMEL

BIENVENIDO AL PARASIO, or in English, WELCOME TO PARADISE.

Settled by the ancient Mayans over two thousand years ago, the Mayan name for Cozumel, is Ah Cuzamil Peten, which translates to Island of the Swallows. The Isle was a shrine to Ixchel, the Mayan goddess of fertility. Mayan women from the mainland were expected to make at least one trip in their life to worship here.

Cozumel now draws thousands of visitors everyday. Known for its world famous dive sites and beautiful white beaches, it is located on the second largest barrier reef system in the world. The Great Mayan Barrier Reef extends from the northern Yucatan to the Honduras. In 1961 Jacques Cousteau discovered the wonders of diving in Cozumel, and declared it one of the greatest dive areas of the world. After that, Cozumel's tourist industry took off and continues to grow larger every year.

Cozumel is a popular cruise ship port with as many as 11 ships docking each day. There is much more than diving on this small island, which measures twenty-eight miles long and ten miles wide. There is much to see and do here. Enjoy water sports, shopping, exploring, or just plain relaxing on the beach with a cold drink and a good book.

One need not be a diver to enjoy what Cozumel has to offer, or to appreciate the warmth and hospitality of the local residents, some of who are direct descendents of the original Mayans. Sit in the Plaza on balmy Sunday evening, listen to the music, dance, and hand out candy to the many young children. You will be rewarded with some of the biggest and brightest smiles you have ever seen.

One visit to Cozumel, and I promise you it will not be your last. On behalf of my friends and the local community of Cozumel, WELCOME!

COZUMEL CALENDER

JANUARY

- New Year's Day (January 1)
  National Holiday.

- Three Kings Day (January 6)
  Christmas continues on through Epiphany, which is called Dia de Los Reyes or Three Kings Day and to Mexican children is much more important than December 25. On the eve of Kings Day, the children leave their shoes out in the hopes that they will wake up to find them filled with toys and other treasures, just as the magi came bearing gifts for the newborn infant so long ago.

  Children and adults gather on January 6 to partake of a traditional treat called Rosca de Reyes or kings' bread, which is a crown-shaped sweet bread decorated with "jewels" of candied fruit. Tiny plastic baby Jesus figures are hidden in the dough before baking and custom dictates that whoever gets a piece of bread containing a baby is responsible to host another party on Candlemas, February 2.

FEBRUARY

- Constitution Day (February 5)
  Speeches and ceremonies commemorating this National Holiday.

- Carnaval: The week preceding Ash Wednesday is a constant party. Celebrates the approaching of Lent with parades, fireworks, food, music and dancing.

Carnaval Royalty

MARCH

- Benito Juarez's Birthday (March 21)
  National Holiday honoring president and leader of the 19th-Century
  Reform movement. Vernal Equinox.

- Late March
  Visitors come to the main temple at Chichen Itza to see the descent of the
  serpent Kukulkan. History has it that the Maya constructed the temple in
  a way that during equinox a beam of sunlight creates a shadow moving
  down towards earth resembling a slithering snake. This occurrence is
  supposed to bring out a good harvest.

APRIL

- Holy Week (April 17th and Easter April 20th)
  Celebrations and processions in observance of Christ's resurrection. Feast
  of El Cedral Late April, Early May. Feast in honor of the founding of
  Cozumel.

- El Cedral Festival (~ April 23rd–May 3rd)

  This sacred holiday begins on April 23rd with a prayer vigil at dawn,
  followed by daily morning and evening novenas leading up to May 3rd.
  On that day, the faithful perform the solemn baile de las cabezas de
  cochino, which literally translates to dance of the pigs' heads. The heads

are a sacrificial offering to God in that He was the first to sacrifice for his people through his suffering on the cross.

For 154 years the Holy Cross Festival has continued to be the heart of what is now a larger non-religious festival called La Feria del Cedral. Descendants continue to participate annually in the Baile de las Cabezas de Cochino, enjoy a wide variety of activities, including sports and cultural events, rodeos, folkloric dancing, live music and horse racing.

MAY

- Cinco de Mayo (May 5)
  National holiday commemorating Mexico's defeat of the French in the Battle of Puebla in 1862.

- Cozumel's International Billfish Tournament
  Competitors from around the world compete in the waters of the Gulf.

SEPTEMBER

- Mexico's Independence Day (September 16)
  Viva Mexico! Mexico celebrates its independence from Spain in 1821. This national celebration is observed here in Cozumel with a grand fireworks display in front of the Municipal Building on Raphael Melgar. There will be countless types of local cuisine in the nearby food court as well as games and rides for the kids.

- Autumnal Equinox (Late September)
  Visitors come to the main temple at Chichen Itza to see the descent of the serpent Kukulkan. History has it that the Maya constructed the temple in a way that during equinox a beam of sunlight creates a shadow moving down towards earth resembling a slithering snake. This occurrence is supposed to bring out a good harvest.

- Feast of San Miguel (September 29)

- Feast of San Miguel, patron saint of the island.

NOVEMBER

- Dia de Los Muertos—Day of the Dead (November 2)
  More than 500 years ago, when the Spanish conquistadors landed in what is now Mexico, they encountered natives practicing a ritual that seemed to mock death. The ritual is known today as Dia de Los Muertos or Day of the Dead and is celebrated throughout Mexico. Today people don wooden skull masks called "cacaos" and dance in honor of their deceased relatives. The wooden skulls are also placed on altars that are dedicated to the dead. A relative or a friend may munch on sugar skulls, made with the names of the dead person on the forehead.

- Anniversary of the Mexican Revolution (November 20)
  Celebration of the Mexican Revolution of 1910 with parades, speeches and ceremonies

DECEMBER

- Festival de Guadalupe—The Virgin of Guadalupe (December 12)
  December 12 is arguably the most important day of the year for millions of Catholics across Mexico as they honor a figure that is considered to be the centerpiece of the Catholic faith in their country.

Festival de Guadalupe

- Las Posadas—Christmas (December 16)
  Christmas festivities begin December 16 with Las Posadas (the inns) and continue for nine days, symbolizing the nine months that Mary carried the baby Jesus in her womb.

  In colonies throughout Cozumel, neighbors, families and church groups gather to reenact the journey of the holy family as they traveled from Nazareth to Bethlehem, seeking shelter on the eve of the savior's birth. The modern-day parade of pilgrims stop at designated houses to sing their request for shelter while those waiting behind the closed door respond with a musical refrain, telling them they have no room

- La Rama (December 16)
  As with most customs in Mexico, La Rama was born out of Indian ritual and in this case is an extension of an Aztec ceremony commemorating the rebirth of nature.
  Officially starting December 16, it generally involves self-organized groups of children who decorate a branch from a tree or plant and then go from door to door shouting "cantamos la rama?" (Can we sing the branch?). Carrying homemade lanterns and accompanied by a rhythm section of kitchen utensils, the groups launch song, always including some verses that ask the audience to give them their aguinaldo (a sort of Christmas bonus) if they are pleased with the performance.

  This continues until just before Christmas eve, when the children give their earnings to one of the children's mothers, which they will use to buy piñatas and treats for their own Christmas party.

CHAPTER I

GENERAL INFORMATION

The basics you need to know.

GENERAL INFORMATION

ENTRY REQUIREMENTS: The Government of Mexico requires that all U.S. citizens present proof of citizenship and photo identification for entry into Mexico. Some U.S. citizens have encountered difficulty in boarding flights in Mexico without a passport. The U.S. Embassy recommends traveling with a valid U.S. passport to avoid delays or misunderstandings. Currently U.S. citizenship documents such as a certified copy (not a photocopy) of a U.S. birth certificate, a Naturalization Certificate, a Consular Report of Birth Abroad, or a Certificate of Citizenship are acceptable. U.S. citizens boarding flights to Mexico should be prepared to present one of these documents as proof of U.S. citizenship, along with photo identification. Driver's permits, voter registration cards, affidavits and similar documents are not sufficient to prove citizenship for readmission into the United States. Passports will be required effective December 2006.

U.S. Consulate Ann R. Harris, Consular Agent
Plaza Villa Mar en El Centro, Plaza Principal, (Parque Juarez between Melgar and 5th Ave.) 2nd floor, Locales #8 and 9, telephone (52)(987) 872-4574.

Police Emergency—01 800 903 9200. If need to talk to someone who speaks English, dial 060 and say "Necesito hablar a un persona que comprender inglais." Routine—Main station is at Melgar between Gonzalo Guerrero & Calle 13; 872-0409

Language: English is widely spoken in Cozumel, but Spanish is the official language. A small percent still speak some Mayan on the island.

Water Temp: The water temperature averages 77 degrees Fahrenheit in the winter and 85 in summer. Although these temperatures sound warm and cozy, a light to medium wetsuit or skin may be needed.

Time Zone: Cozumel is on the Central time zone.

Documents: Proof of citizenship, valid photo ID, and Temporary Tourist card.

WEATHER: Cozumel has two primary seasons. Rainy season, which is mid May to mid October, and dry season the rest of the year. Do not let rainy season keep you away, as they seldom have a rainy day as we know it. Usually a short shower or two and the sun is right back out. Temperatures are warm here all year long ranging from the nineties to the low seventies, seldom dropping below seventy on a cool winter evening. Humidity is similar to what is experienced in Florida with higher humidly in the summer months.

CLOTHING: Please ladies; remember that bathing suits belong at the beach and pool and not on public streets. Cozumel is a very family oriented community and the locals frown on extensive displays of bare flesh anywhere other than at water side.

Light cotton clothing is best suited to the climate here. You will need little more than shorts, tee shirts and bathing suits. A nice pair of slacks and a collared shirt for the men, and a skirt or dress pants for the ladies should be packed. You will want these if you plan to dine at one of the fancier restaurants, to attend church, or if you are invited by a local to some special event. A light jacket or sweater for a cool evening, and a sweatshirt for after diving. Add pair of sandals and a pair of sneakers and you have everything you need.

MEDICAL: Cozumel has excellent clinics and hospitals, good Doctors who speak English, dentists, and even a chiropractor. Please refer to Chapter 10 for names and phone numbers of medical providers.

TIPPING: When tipping or not, please remember that the minimum wage in Mexico is around five or six dollars a day. The workers in the Cozumel service industry depend on tips to support their families.

Waiters/waitresses: Ten to twenty percent of your check depending on quality of service. If gratuity is already included, consider leaving an additional small tip, such as the remaining pesos from your change.

Maids: two to three dollars a day left on your pillow each morning, ensures that the maid who is on duty gets the tip. If you are staying at a small hotel or B&B where it is always the same maid, you can tip at the end of your stay. I do not recommend this because if you tip daily your maid will appreciate it, and you will be amazed at the extra service above and beyond what is expected. Another thing that I and many other frequent visitors do is to leave small gifts with the tips. Dollar store items are great, a small pack of crayons and coloring book for her children, small sample cosmetics, soap, etc for the maid. They really welcome these gifts and you will receive outstanding service. At all inclusive, they may tell you that tips are included, please consider tipping anyway.

Dive and Fishing charters: Ten to fifty dollars per trip, depending on the number in your party. Remember that the tips are shared among the crew.

Taxi Drivers: It is not necessary to tip these drivers, but as inexpensive as the cab fares are, what's another dollar. Again you will get a big smile and a Gracias from the driver.

BANKING AND SHOPPING: Bank and currency exchanges are normally open from nine to five. ATMs are twenty-four hour access. See chapter 10 for locations. Stores usually open about eight in the morning and stay open to very late at night. Siesta time is still practiced at some of the stores further from downtown and may be closed from one to five. See chapter 6 for shopping tips and locations.

EXCHANGE RATE: The rate has stayed between 10 and 11 pesos to the U.S. dollar for several years. Safe calculation is 10 to 1.

POST OFFICE: Located on Ave Rafael Melger and calle 7, it is open Monday to Friday 9-6, and on Saturday 9-12. You can mail your post cards here, but do it the first few days, as you will more than likely beat it home. You also can send telegrams here.

SHIPPING: Pakmail located at 10th Ave # 99 can pack and ship items home for you. Also if for some reason you need something mailed to you while in Cozumel, Fed Ex, UPS, and DHL all have express service to Cozumel.

CELL PHONE USE

In order to use your cellular phone on the Cozumel, Cancun and throughout Quintana Roo, and the Yucatan you must first contact your cell phone company and tell them you are going to Mexico and that you will require International Calling. You can purchase one month's worth.

CHURCH: There are three Catholic Churches, a Christian Non-Denominational, a 7th Day Adventist, and several other churches on the island. See Chapter 10 Special services for more information.

PHONES: You have several options for calling home from Mexico. There are many calling stations, which usually have the best rates. You can use your own cell phone, check with your carrier, they often have plans you can add for a few dollars to enable you to call and receive calls in Mexico. You can buy calling cards. Do not call home collect or make calls from your hotel, the charges will put you into shock.

LAUNDRY: There are Laundromats all over Cozumel. You can do it yourself or use drop off service. They will wash, dry, and fold in about two hours. I do not know what they use, but it smells so good. We usually drop off the day before we leave, and go home with all clean clothes.

GAS STATIONS: There are now three stations on the Isle. Juarez and 30th Ave, Juarez and 75th Ave, and the new one across from Puerto Maya. Be sure to get out of your car immediately and see them reset the pump to zero. A few dishonest station attendants have been known to charge extra, by not resetting the pump. A small tip to the attendant is appropriate.

Childcare: Most hotels offer babysitters with advance notice. If you are staying in a Villa, the management will arrange Spanish or English speaking caregivers for $5–7.

If you get cheated by a merchant of any type:
Contact PROFECO (MX federal bureau of consumer protection) at the big white Municipal Building (Palacio) on Melgar, or through:
http://www.profeco.gob.mx/html/consumidor/denuncias.htm#attention

CHAPTER II

GETTING THERE

Check out your options for travel.

GETTING THERE

There are only two ways in which to arrive in Cozumel, by air or water. Most visitors that arrive by water are passengers one of the many cruise ships that arrive daily at one of three cruise piers. These tourists get to sample Cozumel for a few short hours, but it is this small taste that often brings them back by plane for a longer stay.

The others that arrive by water are passengers on either the people ferries, or the car ferry. It is possible to drive your own vehicle to Cozumel for an extended visit, but you will have to bring it across on the car ferry out of Calica, near Playa del Carmen. The cost for the car ferry is approximately $45.00.

The passengers on the two people ferries from Playa del Carmen have usually flown into Cancun and either taken the bus or a van to Playa del Carmen. This is a popular option as there are many better airfare deals into Cancun, then there are into Cozumel Of course you can fly directly into the Cozumel airport via several Commercial carriers and several charter carriers.

Taxi-cabs are only allowed to drop off at the airport, but not allowed to pick up. You will have to take a Collectivo van at a cost of $5.00–$20.00 and will make many stops. If you would like to save and take a taxi, just walk out of the airport and across the street where you can easily flag one down.

AIRLINES SERVING COZUMEL

Aero Mexico	www.aeromexico.com	1-800-237-6639
American Airlines	www.aa.com	1-800-433-7300
Continental Airlines	www.continental.com	1-800-523-3273
Delta Airlines	www.delta.com	1-800-221-1212
Mexicana Air	www.mexicana.com	1-800531-7921
Northwest Air	www.nwa.com	1-800-225-2525

Spirit Airlines   www.spiritair.com   1-800-772-7117
Serves only Cancun, but great prices.

Sun Country air   www.suncountry.com   1-800-359-6786

U S Airways   www.usairways.com   1-800-622-1015

United Airlines   www.united.com   1-800-864-8331

CHARTERS

Adventure Tours   www.atusa.com   1-800-642-8872.

Funjet Vacations   www.funjet.com   1-866-558-6654

Worry-free Vacations www.worryfreevacations.com 1-888-225-5658

DISCOUNT AIRFARES

Sky Auction   www.skyauction.com
  You can often get a very good deal at this site. I have used them without any problem.

Fly Cheap Abroad wwww.flycheapabroad.com
  I have found my best fares at this site. You may have to play with your dates.

Latin Discount Air www.latindiscountair.com
  Have some very good fares.

CANCUN AIRPORT BUS SCHEDUAL-RIVIERA BUS/FERRY TO COZUMEL

If you find a great fare into Cancun, by all means grab it. The transportation to Playa del Carmen by bus and then to Cozumel by ferry is easy and reasonable. Buses are comfortable and air-conditioned. Trip takes approximately 45 minutes to Playa.

BUS SCHEDUAL   Fare is $65 pesos or $7.00

Cancun to Playa del Carmen: 10:45am, 11:45am, 12:45pm, 1:45pm, 3:00pm, 4:45pm, 7:00pm, 8:30pm

Playa del Carmen to Cancun: 8:00am, 9:00am, 10:30am, 11:45am, 1:00pm, 3:00pm, 4:00pm, 5:00pm, 6:15pm

FERRY SCHEDUAL   Fare is approximately $11.00 each way

Playa del Carmen to Cozumel: 6:00am then every hour on the hour 8:00am–9:00pm and 11:00pm

Cozumel to Playa del Carmen: Every hour on the hour 5:00am–8:00pm and 10:00pm
No 1 pm ferry

Vehicle Ferry:

Calica to Cozumel: Monday-Saturday 2:00am, 7:00am, 11:00am, 3:00pm, 5:00pm, 9:00pm

Sunday 7:00am, 1:00pm, 5:00pm, 9:00pm

Cozumel to Calica: Monday and Saturday 4:30am, 9:00am, 1:00pm, 3:00pm, 7:00pm, 12:00am

Sunday 4:30am, 9:00am, 3:00pm, 7:00pm

TIP: At the bus station and ferry terminals you will see men on large tricycles. They are called tricyclo men and will take all your luggage to the ferry, or from the ferry. No set cost, just tip him well.

CHAPTER III

WHERE TO STAY

You have many choices for lodging in Cozumel.

WHERE TO STAY

Lodging options in Cozumel range from small family run hotels and B&Bs to all-inclusive mega resorts where you never have to leave the property during vacation. It would be a shame to choose the latter and never get a chance to experience the true flavor of Cozumel. We recommend that even if you stay at an all-inclusive property, that you still venture into town to shop, eat dinner at a local restaurant, and mingle with the people. I promise you will not be disappointed.

Another wonderful option is to rent a casa or villa. Become part of the neighborhood, meet the neighbors, shop at the Mercado and experiment with Mexican food and recipes in your own kitchen. Relax at your own private pool without a crowd, even go skinny-dipping if you would like.

When you rent a villa or casa, it is often less than the cost of a hotel room if the cost is shared with others. Maid service is included and you can even hire a cook for your stay. Whichever you choose, relax and enjoy your Cozumel vacation.

BED AND BREAKFASTS

ALICIA'S B & B   www.gis.net/~alicia
65th Ave y 65 bis y calle 19   1-866-511-1014 1-832-615-9254

Located in a residential neighborhood, close to local stores and restaurants Just a brisk 15-minute walk to downtown or a $2–3 cab ride. The new bus service runs right by here and you can go to the beach for $20 pesos.

Operated by Alicia, an American expatriate and her Mayan partner Chuco, they will have you believing you are just part of the family. Chuco is also the cook here and his breakfasts are awesome, they alone are worth the price charged for a night. His guacamole is the best on the island.

There is no pool here, but who needs it with all the wonderful beaches and beach clubs that are available in paradise. All rooms have refrigerators, ceiling fans, and

AC. There is a coffee maker, BBQ grill and area for light cooking. For divers there is a large rinse tank for your gear. Talk shop with Chuco as he used to be a dive boat captain, and loves to practice his English. I have stayed with Alicia many times and whole heartedly can recommend this B & B.

Large rooms $40.00 per night for 2. $5 additional person
Small room with 2 singles $25 for 1 and $5 additional person. Tax is included.

I have stayed with Alicia many times, as have a lot of others. Once a customer, always a friend.

AMIGO'S BED AND BREAKFAST
Calle 7 #571 between Aves 25 and 30

www.bacalar.net
011-52-987-872-3868

This cute B&B consists of three cottage style rooms with palapa roofs, set in a tropical garden. Each room has a private bath and kitchenette. A continental breakfast of coffee, tea, juices, fresh fruit, cereals, and pastries is included. It is within easy walking distance to shopping and downtown interests and restaurants. Nice swimming pool area, bikes available for guests.

May 1–Aug 31	$50.00 double	$10 for additional person
Sep 1–Oct 31	$40.00 double	$10 for additional person
Nov 1–Dec 18	$50.00 double	$10 additional person
Jan 8–april 30	$65.00 double	$10 additional person

Inquire for Holiday rates

B & B CARIBO
Corner of Juarez and Ave 40

www.cozumel.net/bb/caribo
011-52-987-872-3195

This is a small B&B offering Yoga vacations. Serves full American breakfasts, but also offers vegetarian dishes. Roof top garden with beautiful view. Close to downtown restraints, local movie theater and shopping. No pool, but easy access to beaches.

Room and Breakfast   Dec 25–Easter $50.00 double
                       Easter–Dec 24 $35.00 double

Yoga Vacation includes breakfast/dinner $249.00 single $319.00 double per week tax included

BALDWINS GUEST HOUSE   www.moos epages.com
Ave 55 between calle 1 and Salas Ave   011-52-987-872-1148

Dale and Kathy, a very warm and friendly couple, own this wonderful little B&B. Set behind an 8 ft privacy wall you will find a small piece of paradise among the beautiful flowers and fruit trees. Beautifully decorated rooms, a casita, and a 3-bedroom house are available for your stay. A large pool area, outdoor kitchen and an entertainment gazebo provide for all your needs. Relax in a hammock with a good book, or for a peaceful siesta. A full breakfast is served each morning.

Rates range from $75.00–150.00 double

CHARRITTA'S COZUMEL BED AND BREAKFAST   www.cozumelbandb.com
Calle 11

This is a lovely 5 bedroom B&B located on a main street in San Miguel. Owned and operated by Sandy Gutierrez a former Continental Airlines employee, she definitely brings her people skills with her to the B&B. Rooms are large, airy and each distinctly and beautifully decorated. Rooms have private balconies, there is a roof top patio and a tropical courtyard garden. A large filling Mayan breakfast is included.
No pool, but easy access to beaches. Easy walking distance to shopping and restaurants.

Rates start at $26.50 per person + 12% tax

LAS LUNAS INN BED AND BREAKFAST
Ave 40 # 265 between calle 6 & 4

www.laslunas.com
011-52-987-872-5235

A small B&B catering to scuba divers. The owners are Oliver and Jamie Robertson, a couple with a passion for diving. Rooms are basic, but roomy and comfortable. Consists of 2 rooms, with shared bath, and a casita with private bath and refrigerator. No pool, but who cares, if you will be diving every day. A continental breakfast of fresh fruit, pastries, and cereals is included. Open December thru April only, as the owners spend the rest of the year diving. Rooms $30.00 double Casita $45.00 double

SUMMER PLACE INN
Ave 10 #1119 between calle 17 & 19

www.cozumelbedandbreakfast.com
011-52-987-872-6300

A large beautiful B&B. Rooms are large and spacious and beautifully decorated. Large pool for swimming or just floating and relaxing. Breakfast is self-serve and there is a fully stocked refrigerator available 24 hours a day. Beautiful gardens, and hammocks for siesta. Equipment storage and rinse tank, bikes, and wave boards are available. Located two blocks from the ocean, and easy access to shopping and dining. Laundry is available on site.

Can be rented by the room, or the entire complex. Total occupancy is 18.

April 1–Dec 15 $65.00 double $450.00 week $3000 entire complex
Dec 15–April 1 $85.00 double $595.00 week $4000.00 entire complex

TAMARINDO'S BED AND BREAKFAST
Calle 4 between Ave 20 y 25

www.cozumel.net/bb/tamarind
011-52-987-872-3614

Hosted by a friendly couple, Eliane and Jorge, they will be happy to assist you anyway they can. A small nicely decorated B&B with 5 rooms, each having private bath and cable TV and ceiling fans. Only 2 rooms have AC, but the ceiling fans cool nicely.

Breakfast is prepared and served by Eliane with a clearly French influence, as Eliane is from Normandy, France. Her breakfasts are enough to hold you well until lunch. Wireless internet connection is available, so bring your laptop. An easy walk to downtowns shopping and dining. No pool.

Jorge and Eliane also have another unusual property, which I have stayed in with my sons. Palapas Amaranto, 3 Mayan huts and a tower with 2 studio apartments. It has a mini wading pool to cool off in. No breakfast.

Prices at both B&B and Palapas Amaranto run from $41.00–$57.00 tax included

ECONOMY HOTELS

HOTEL AGUILAR   www.cozumel-hotels.net/aguilar
Ave 3 #98   haguilar@coznet.finred.com.mx
In town   011-52-987-872-0307

A small basic hotel popular with divers and those on a budget. Located just one block from the pier and three blocks from the Plaza. An easy stroll for shopping, dining, and dive boat pick-ups.

All rooms have AC, ceiling fans refrigerator, and TVs are available for a fee. Rooms are very basic with two double beds, nightstand, and dresser. Most important is that they are kept very clean. Nice pool area for after diving relaxation.

$34.00–$48.00 double

BAHIA HOTEL   www.cozumel-hotels.net/bahia
Melger Ave & Calle 3
Down town 27 rooms

If you are here purely for the diving and do not need a lot of extras, this is the place. Just 20 steps from the down town piers, makes it very convenient for dive boat pickups. Rooms are large, bright and comfortable, furnished with either a king size bed or a king and a double. Rooms include AC, ceiling fans, satellite

TV, and kitchenettes. Request one of the ocean front rooms that are on each floor, some have balconies. Right in the center of Cozumel's best shopping and dining. A continental breakfast of coffee, pastries and fresh fruit is included.

Rates start at $45 double

HOTEL BELLO CARIBE   email bcaribe@prodigy.net.mx
#660 Pedro Joaquin Coldwell Ave   011-52-987-872-6520
In Town 40 rooms

Small family hotel located only 3 minutes from the airport, making it great for those early morning flights. The rooms are good sized and decorated in pretty pastels and bamboo. There is a large pool area and tropical gardens for your enjoyment. They have a deal which is hard to beat, called the BBB plan, which is bed, breakfast, and bike for $38.00 a night.

HOTEL BARRACUDA   www.cozumel-hotels.net/barracuda
628 Rafael Melger Ave   barracudahotelczm@prodigy.net.mx
Down town/Ocean front   1-866-327-1389
52 rooms   011-52-987-872-0002

Everything a diver could want at an economical price. Good shore diving from the hotel beach, private pier for pick up, Dive Paradise dive shop on site and even lockers for your gear, but be sure to bring your own lock. Rooms are simply furnished but large and roomy, with AC, ceiling fans, and refrigerator. TV is $2 additional. The rooms above the first floor have small balconies with awesome Caribbean views. Dining, shopping, and nightclubs are a short walk from the hotel. Shop for your essentials, drinks and snacks from Chedraui's or enjoy a show at the cinema, both a 2-minute stroll across the street.

$58:00–$89.00 double

CASITA de MAYA

Ave 65 & Aero Puerto
Airport 4 rooms

www.casitademaya.com
info@casitademaya.com
011-52-987-879-2606

Gives a new meaning to "Airport hotel", this awesome new addition to the Cozumel lodging scene is literally steps away from the airport. The only thing lacking here are additional rooms, but then that is part of what makes it special. All four rooms are poolside, brand new and tastefully furnished. Amenities include a small refrigerator, hair dryer, microwave, alarm clock, and internet connection for your laptop. There is even a small "dive bar" where you can relax with a cold cervasa while watching big screen TV. Island Dan is the American owner, who will go out of his way to help you with rental cars, tours, directions, he will even meet you at the air port with a cold cervasa. What more could you ask for? Worth the rack rates and more!

$59–$79 double

HOTEL COLONIAL

Ave 5 & Calle 3
Down town on Plaza
28 rooms and suites

www.suitescolonial.com
reservaciones@suitescolonial.com
1-877-228-6747
011-52-987-872-9090

The hottest place in town for people watching. This may be a small hotel, but it offers nice rooms and amenities. The balcony looks straight down into the plaza, which gives you a front row seat for the Sunday evening activities and a good view of Carnaval happenings. Be sure to book way ahead if you want a room during Carnaval. Rooms and suites are simply decorated, but large and well equipped with AC, refrigerator, and TV. Suites have living room and kitchenette. Decent pool area to relax in. Includes a continental breakfast served each morning in the lobby. Internet access also available in lobby.

$49.00–$81.00 double

HOTEL COSTA BRAVA
601 Rafael Melger
In Town

www.cozumel-hotels.net/costa_brava
cosbrava@prodigy.net.mx
011-52-987-872-1290

Welcome to the Hacienda! This will be your first thought as you arrive at the hotel. A small hotel built in traditional hacienda style architecture, with a beautiful garden and palapa area. A BBQ is set up in the garden so that you can grill what you catch. Small, basic, but very clean rooms with AC and cable TV in each room. Gourmet Mexican restaurant, Mexico En los Siglos, on site. Within easy walking distance to shopping and dining. Beach access across the street at the Barracuda hotel. Mega value for your dollar.

$38.00–$45.00 double

DAYS INN-VILLA IGUANA
460 Ave 11
In Town 43 rooms

www.daysinn.com
011-52-987-872-1600

Good value for your money. A typical Days Inn, just set in paradise. Located on a main street, a short walk to dining and shopping. Standard chain hotel rooms, but clean and adequate. Clean fresh water pool. Restaurant on site serves a nice breakfast.

Rates begin at $45.00 double

HOTEL DEL CENTRO
501 Juarez Ave

hcentro@cozumel.com.mx
011-52-987-872-5471

Small basic local hotel with small simple rooms. All rooms have AC. Small pool area with lounge chairs. Sometimes gets noisy from the streets, but if AC is running you will not hear it. Short 5-block walk to the Plaza.

$45.00–$85.00

HOTEL EL MARQUES

no web site or email

180 Ave 5

011-52-987-872-0677

In Town 40 rooms

Almost part of the Plaza square it is so close. Small clean local hotel with fair sized rooms that are simply decorated. All have AC, which will mute the noise from the Plaza and street. A friendly smiling staff and night watchman. Terrific location for access to dining and shopping. No pool area.

$44.00 double includes tax

EL PIRETA

Ave 5 between calle 1 & Salas

Small local hotel—not reviewed.

$22.00 double w/fan $28.00 double w/AC

HOTEL FLAMINGO

www.hotelflamingo.com

Calle 6

info@hotelflamiggo.com

In Town 22 rooms

1-800-806-1601

011-52-987-872-1264

The American owner of this old time Mexican hotel is presently making improvements to the property. It is already a good value and the changes will only make it a better one. Tom has recently added a new chef to his staff, who is cooking Chilean dishes and getting rave reviews. The rooms are clean, large and basically furnished. Each has 2 double beds, ceiling fans, AC and refrigerators are presently being added to each room. Centrally located 1-½ blocks from the heart of town, it is an easy walk to dining and shopping. This is also one of the few properties that has rooms with good wheelchair access, including roll in showers.

$59.00–$89.00 double

Hotel Flamingo

HOTEL KAREY   011-52-987-872-2011
Ave 25 & Salas
In Town

Small local hotel with very basic but clean rooms. Rooms have ceiling fans but AC is extra. Has a small pool and courtyard.

$275 MP (app $27) Fan $300 MP (app $30) AC

HOTEL LETTY   011-52-987-872-0257
Calle 1 & Ave 15
In Town

Small local hotel with basic rooms, ceiling fans, no AC. First floor rooms are light and airy. Just a short walk t the Plaza, dining, and shopping. Run by very warm and friendly family.

$200 MP (app $20.00)

HOTEL MARY CARMEN
4 Ave 5
In Town 30 rooms

011-52-987-872-0581
1-866-613-9330

Small Mexican hotel owned an operated by a nice family. Clean basic rooms with cold AC. Close to shopping, dining and nightlife.

$35.00–$45.00

MAYA COZUMEL
4 Calle 5
In Town 42 rooms

011-52-987-872-0011

Located down town and close to everything, shopping, dining, and dive piers. Clean comfortable rooms with Ac. Nice pool area to relax at.

$25.00–$50.00

HOTEL MESON SAN MIGUEL
Ave Juarez On Plaza
Plaza 96 rooms

www.mesonsanmiguel.com
info@mesonsanmiguel.com
011-52-987-872-0233

This hotel's location right on the main plaza and the low rates make this a bargain. Rooms are medium sized, clean and simply decorated, with most rooms over looking the Plaza or the pool area. All rooms have Ac and cable TV. Suites are larger with nice sitting area. Request the top floor and be rewarded with a great ocean view. Small pool and sun bathing area.

$40.00–$80.00

PALMA DORADA INN
011-52-987-872-0330
#44 A.R. Salas Ave

Small basic family run hotel. Adequate size rooms, clean and simple. Staff is very friendly. Offers free pastries and coffee in the morning. Close to dining and shopping.

$30.00 double/fan $43.00 double/AC

HOTEL PEPITA
011-52-987-872-0098
#120 Ave 15
In Town 20 rooms

Good choice for people on a budget, or wanting to spend their dollars on more important things. Clean basic rooms with showers, AC, cable TV, no phone. Five minute walk to the main plaza for shopping and dining. Enjoy a round of mini golf and a sangria at Cozumel Mini golf right down the street. No pool

$30.00 double

PLAZA COZUMEL
www.hotelplazacozumel.com
#3 Calle 2 (½ block to waterfront)
In Town 61 rooms

This has got to be one of the best-kept secrets on Cozumel. This budget hotel has roof top pool and bar with an amazing Caribbean ocean view, not what you would expect at their prices. Small but clean and brightly decorated rooms with AC and cable TV. Just steps away from the museum which you should not miss, and close to the Plaza, shopping, dining, and piers.

$50.00 double

POSADA EDEM
011-52-987-872

Calle 2 between Ave 5 & 10

Small family hotel, with small functional rooms decorated in pink. Some rooms have AC. Close to Plaza and downtown areas for dining and shopping, Friendly staff.

$22.00 double/fan $28.00 double/AC

Punta Morena
http://www.cozumeltravel.com/Restaurants/Punta%20Morena/PuntaMorena.htm
At Punta Morena Beach

All rooms are beachfront.

NO ELECTRICITY. COLD RUNNING WATER ONLY. There is no electricity on this side of the island. Only for the adventurous.

Each room includes 1 bedroom, 1 bathroom with toilet & Shower & COLD running water, 1 Kitchenette including counter space & sink with COLD running water.

$150 mp

MODERATE HOTELS

HOTEL CARIBE BLU
www.cozumel-hotels.net/la-reina

Melger Ave 1 ¼ miles south of town
Ocean Front 22 rooms

This little family run hotel gets 5 star reviews from visitors. Formerly known as the Lorena for you Cozumel old timers. A sunset performance that is unforgettable. The shore is a rocky front, not a sandy beach, but do not let this stop you from enjoying some great snorkeling and diving only steps from your doorway. On site is Blue Angel Dive shop and a small restaurant serving breakfast and lunch. There is a nice size fresh water pool. Rooms are furnished with 2 double or 1 king bed, and have a balcony to watch the sunset from. TV, safe, AC, and phone are standard. A brisk walk or short cab ride to town.

Rates start @ $80.00 double

CASA DEL MAR
Melger Ave 2 ½ miles south of town
Ocean View 98 rooms/8 cabanas

www.casadelmarcozumel.com
reservations@casadelmar.com

A Howard Johnson's type hotel with a few extra frills. The views of the Caribbean sunsets are the best thing about this property. Rooms are clean, basic, middle class Mexico. Reserve one of the 2 story cabanas if you can, they come with a small kitchenette. Pool area is nice, but beach area across the street is small, nearly non-existent. You do get the use of Nachi Com a very nice beach club further south. The breakfast here is reported to be excellent, but other meals receive mixed reviews. Good deals are to be found on the internet that will be way below the listed rack rates.

Rack Rates $99.00–$209.00

CASA MEXICANA
#457 Melger Ave
Down town water front—90 rooms

WWW.CASAMEXICANACOZUMEL.COM
reservaciones@casaamericanacozumel.com
1-877-228-6747/011-52-987-872-9073

WOW! This modern Mexican architecture stands out, yet seems to belong. One of the newer additions to Cozumel's inventory of hotels, the building was awarded 1st place by Modern Mexican Architecture's regional biennial for Design. The furnishings are outstanding, beds, desks, and all wooden furniture are hand carved Mayan wood.
Enjoy sunbathing at the pool on the second story while gazing out at the Caribbean sea, beautiful on a star lit night. During the day you can watch the cruise ships come and go. There is also an indoor pool with poolside bar. Rooms have balconies, TV, phone, refrigerator, and even plush bathrobes. Definitely first class for a good price. Breakfast buffet is included and served on the terrace.

$115–165 double check internet for great deals

HOTEL COZUMEL
North beach Zone
AI Option 180 rooms

www.hotelcozumel.us
1-877-454-4355
011-52-987-872-2855

Home to Cozumel's largest swimming pool, this pool is huge with what seems like miles of lounge chairs surrounding it. There is also a second smaller pool and Jacuzzi. Rooms are nice enough, comparable to a Holiday Inn, but with plenty of space and nice large balconies. Be sure to request an ocean front room.
Snorkeling and diving from the rocky beach is lots of fun, as you will see a large assortment of marine life. Dive Paradise is the on site dive operator, with boats leaving from the private pier. The hotel has recently added an all-inclusive option and the food reviews have run from adequate to amazing. Breakfast getting the highest marks. You can take the AI plan, eat breakfast and lunch there, but eat out at night, and this should still give you a good deal.

Rates start at $100 double and $75 PP if AI Again…check the internet for bargains

EL CID LA CEIBA
South Zone Beach Front
Near Puerto Maya 71 rooms

www.elcid.com
cozumel@elcid.com.mx
1-800-435-3240
011-52-987-872-0844

A long time favorite of the wet suit crowd, offers excellent dive packages. This property seems to get mixed reviews, either they love it or hate it, so judge for yourself and read the reviews. Located directly in front of a cruise pier, the ships can block the views from some of the rooms. Time-share presentations seem to be a priority here. If you are not interested, just say *"no gracias"* and keep walking. Rooms are quite large and beautifully decorated, and come with small balconies which are handy for drying dive gear. All rooms have AC, satellite TV, and VCR, with movie rentals available at the front desk. There is a dive operation on site, two pools, a small sandy beach, and a fitness center. Request a tower room, these have been recently renovated and have incredible views.

Rates start at $110.00 double AI option is available. Check internet for sales.

FIESTA AMERICANA DIVE RESORT
South Zone Beach across the street
228 rooms AI option

www.fiestaamericana.com
1-800-FIESTA-1
011-52-987-872-9600

The biggest selling point for this property is the location, near some of the best reefs for diving and snorkeling. Rooms are good sized, and some of them have good ocean views. Avoid the casitas, it is a very long walk to the beach and pool from them, and there have been complaints of excessive bugs, probably due to their proximity to the jungle. The pool area is very nice and they have some of the most beautiful tropical gardens on Cozumel. Dive House is the dive operation on site. Chankanaab Park is a short walk from the hotel.

Rates start @ $95.00 double AI option is $55.00 additional per person

HACIENDA SAN MIGUEL
#500 Calle 10
In Town

www.haciendasanmiguel.com
info@haciendasanmiguel.com
1-866-712-6387
011-52-987-872-1986

Absolutely stunning old Mexico, both inside and out. Rooms are large and beautiful decorated with Mexican art work. Studios, Jr suites, and a town house all come with kitchen or kitchenette. Located close to the Plaza and it is close to dining and shopping. There is no swimming pool, but there is a beautiful and peaceful fountain area and garden, perfect for some quiet time, or reading a good book. A continental breakfast is served in your room each morning, and at night you just may receive a treat of homemade cookies. Staff is friendly and treat you as part of the family.

$95.00–$156.00

REEF CLUB COZUMEL
South Zone Beach Front
ALL INCLUSIVE 240 rooms

www.reefclubcozumel.com
reefclubcozumel@prodigy.net.mx
1-888-773-4349
011-52-987-872-9300

Set on a nice beach, this property consists of three story Caribbean style bungalows, which house spacious suites and studios. Single story bungalows contain the standard hotel rooms, which are plenty spacious. All are decorated in pretty soft pastels. All rooms have balconies or terraces to sit on and enjoy the ocean breezes, and the sweet smell of the jungle. For the diver there is Sand Dollar Sports on site, whose dive boats leave directly from the hotel pier. The buffets and snack bars are of the usual AI quality, some good, some not so good. There is a reservation only restaurant, but I have been told it is often difficult to get reservations. Reviews on this property seem to report that customers with VIP status gold bracelets have a better experience.

$84.00–$190.00 PP all inclusive

SCUBA CLUB COZUMEL
Melger Ave 1 mile south of don town
Water front ALL INCLUSIVE

www.scubaclubcozumel.com
1-800-847-5708
011-52-987-872-0853

A great basic and long-time favorite of divers. The rooms are large and simply but pleasantly decorated. All rooms have AC, but TVs are viewed as an interruption of relaxation and diving...so no TV. The food served is the basic AI menus, with an excellent breakfast. Eat your breakfast here, walk to town for dinner, and you will still get a decent deal. Offers excellent dive packages, with dive operator on site.

Rates vary by package and diver/non diver from $296.00 for a 3 night non diving stay based on triple in Sept to $1396.00 for 7 nights/5days diving based on single. Prices are per person

SOL CABANAS del CARIBE
North Zone Beach Front
48 rooms

www.cozumel-hotels.net/sol_cabanas

011-52-987-872-0017

Located on a small white sandy beach just 10 minutes north of town. Consists of standard rooms and 8 cabanas, the cabanas actually being smaller. Standard rooms have terrace or balcony, and small sitting area, cabanas are right next to the pool. All have AC but no TV or phones. A very quiet property, great for a relaxing vacation. Pleasant pool area with palapa for shade, and good snorkeling off the beach.

Rates start @ 75.00 double

Ventanas al Mar Hotel
beach area next to Coconuts

www.cozumel-hotels.net/ventanas-aleast
ventanasalmar@cozumel-hotels.net

A unique Caribbean experience, this oceanfront hotel is located on the east side of Cozumel Island where there is always a breeze and where there are no other hotels. Wind turbines, with storage batteries, use the steady ocean breezes to produce the hotel's electricity. Beautiful cozy rooms, decorations are Mexican Rustic with Talavera accents.
A different experience from the regular hotel stay. Breakfast is included. You really need a rental car if you stay here.

Rates $65–$150

VILLAS LAS ANCLAS
01152 9 8787 25476
325. 5th Ave between 3rd& 5th St

http://lasanclas.com/Index.html

Small, quiet, intimate hotel, made up of spacious suites arranged along a shady, serene tropical garden. Each suite has two floors with living, dining and kitchenette areas on the first floor, and a queen size bedroom with bath on the second floor. No pool.

Rates $80–$120

Vista del Mar
www.cozumel-hotels.net/vistadelmar
info@hotelvistadelmar.com
Waterfront on Melger

1-888-309-9988

Decorated in a cozy elegant Mexican style using wood, shells, mosquito netting and natural materials. Rooms are clean and comfortable with great views. Close to everything. No pool, but has a large Jacuzzi.

Rates $59–$94

EXPENSIVE

ALLEGRO COZUMEL
South Zone Beach Front
ALL INCLUSIVE 300 rooms

www.occidentalhotels.com
1-800-858-2258

Welcome to Gilligans's Island or so you may think when you see the 2 story thatched bungalows. Set on one of the best beach areas on the Isle, San Francisco Beach. Rooms are good sized and nicely furnished. All rooms have balconies or terraces, AC, phone, satellite TV, full baths with tubs. Enjoy the oceanfront Jacuzzi or swim up bar at one of the two pools. Enjoy playing in the crystal blue Caribbean with free kayaks, snorkel gear, boogie boards, and wind surfing. The main dining area is the Topaz, which offers standard AI menu and buffet. Breakfasts are good with made to order omelets, lunches are mediocre. Reservation only at Caruso's (Italian) and La Troje (Mexican) get ratings of fair to good. There are extra charges for steak or lobster meals

Rates start at $284.00 double all inclusive

CORAL PRINCESS
North Zone Beach Front
139 rooms

www.coralprincess.com
reservations@coralprincess.com
1-800-253-2702
011-598872-3200

Set on a private beach about 10 minutes north of town. The pool area a grounds are beautiful with a definite Caribbean feel. The rooms range from a standard room, which I thought were a little tight for space, and one, two, and three bedroom suites. The suites are much roomier. All are decorated beautifully in eye appealing colors. There are two on site restaurants that serve here and reviews were decent. An American breakfast in included for adults. The bars offer 2 for one at happy hour.

Rates $132–$627.00

COZUMEL PALACE
Melger Ave In town
Water Front

www.palaceresorts.com
1-800-635-1836
011-52-987-872-9430

Palace Resorts scores big time with Cozumel's newest addition with this 5 star resort. Previously known as Plaza Las Glorias, the building was totally renovated and recently opened May 2005.

If You want true pampering, 5 star accommodations, and amenities, this is THE place. Every room is ocean view with balcony and Jacuzzi in the room. All new elegant furnishings, quiet AC, ceiling fans, room safe, coffee maker, mini bar, bathrobes and more. Two swimming pools with swim up bar and dive operation is on site. The only negative point is that there is no beach, but the pool is oceanfront. You will be pampered and treated as royalty here. The prices are steep, but good deals can be found on the internet.

Rates start at $278 pp all-inclusive

EL COZUMELENO RESORT
South Zone Beach Front
ALL INCLUSIVE 252 rooms

www.elcozumeleno.com
reserva@elczumeleno.com
1-800-437-3923
011-52-987-872-9530

This property receives high marks for it's large sandy white beach. Beautiful free-form pool with waterfall is a pleasure to spend time at. Snorkeling is good from the beachfront. Activity is never ending here, with a staff that strives to make your vacation fun, you can even play beach bingo. Food is slightly better than the usual all-inclusive fare, but customers report difficulty obtaining tables at the reservation only restaurant.

Rooms are spacious and decorated in pretty pastels, AC is COLD, great after a day in the humidity. Bring your own beach towels here, as they have a $50.00 fee for lost towels.

Rates$85–$195 PP all inclusive

El Cozumeleno Resort

IBEROSTAR RESORT   www.iberostar.com
South Zone Beach Front
ALL INCLUSIVE 306 rooms

This resort has some of the most beautiful grounds on the Isle, well maintained tropical gardens with peacocks and peahens roaming freely, lots of iguanas, and colorful parrots in cages. The beach is a bit of a disappointment, as it is more rocky than sandy. Be sure to bring beach shoes to protect your feet. Rooms are of average size, furnished nicely with all the basic amenities, AC, safe, TV. The AI food is the usual for an AI, with a good breakfast, the other meals acceptable. With Palancar Reef at your door step it is a good place for divers, and there is an on site dive operation.

Rates start at $230.00 double

MELIA COZUMEL   www.meliacozumel.com
North Zone Beach Front   1-888-774-0040
All Inclusive 150 rooms   011-52-987-872-0700

This all inclusive is located on a nice beach about 3 miles north of downtown. The room choices are standard and mini suites, with all rooms having terraces or balconies. Rooms are good sized and decorated in bright Caribbean style and colors. Club Fantasia provides musical entertainment and Mexican shows in the evening, fun for all. The food at this all inclusive gets good marks, and the Reservation only restaurant, Café, Pariso serves up excellent steaks and seafood. Choice of 2 pools, one with a swim up bar. In addition to the usual tennis and non-motorized water sports offered at all inclusive, the Melia also offers horse back riding and Spanish lessons.

Rates start @ $95.00 pp all inclusive

OCCIDENTAL GRAND
South Zone Beach Front
ALL INCLUSIVE 252 rooms

www.grandcozumel.com
1-800-858-2258
011-52-987-872-9730

Located on fabulous San Francisco Beach, with the lush Caribbean jungle set behind it, it is a beautiful property. The grounds are exceptionally manicured and groomed. The large standard rooms are simply but elegantly furnished and decorated, with all the amenities. The walk in showers have plenty of room to hang dive gear, and still have room to shower. The AI food at the buffets are pretty much the same as other AIs, but their other restaurants are very good, be sure to try Los Olivos. Consider renting a car unless you plan to spend all your time at the hotel. It is a $20–$25 cab ride into town. There is a new bus service started summer 2005 that will cost $20 pesos and runs hourly.

Rates start @ $230.00 double

PARK ROYAL
North Zone Across from beach
ALL INCLUSIVE 143 rooms

www.cozumel-hotels.net/park-royal

The outstanding feature at this property is it's large free form swimming pool surrounded by tropical gardens. There is a small island and palapa in the middle of the pool. A short underpass takes you across the street to a secluded cove with a nice beach. All rooms have either an ocean view or a partial ocean and pool view. Rooms are nice size and come with all the normal amenities. Buffets are run of the mill AI, fine for the kids, but adults should stick to the reservation only facility for dinners. Breakfast buffets are good.

Rates $130–$189 pp all inclusive

PLAYA AZULE HOTEL
www.playa-azul.com
North Zone Beach Front
011-52-987-872-0033
90 rooms

This is the only hotel in Cozumel that offers free greens fees at the golf club. Has some great golf packages. All rooms are ocean front with large balconies to view the beautiful ocean. Suites, master suites, and a 3 bedroom garden house are all decked out in bright Mexican colors and furnishings. The hotel has a small sparsely populated sandy white beach has some good snorkeling. Be sure to try the fajitas in the on site restaurant, they are YUMMY.

Rates $130–$350 double

PRESIDENTE INTER-CONTINENTAL www.cozumel.intercontinental.com
South Zone Beach Front
cozumel@interconti.com
253 rooms
1-888-303-1758
011-52-987-872-9500

Located on a beautiful white beach to the south of San Miguel, this lovely property is first class all the way. Beach and beach front pools are a nice place to enjoy a day in the Caribbean, as the waiters serve your every wish. Rooms are very large, understated and elegant. All rooms have balconies or terraces overlooking the ocean. At night you can see the twinkling lights from the main land. There are three dining choices at the hotel, but the newest is Alfredo's, which is getting rave reviews, even from the local chefs.

Rates $176–$595 double

VILLA RENTALS

AT HOME IN COZUMEL
www.cozumel.tc
1-800-833-5971

Rents ocean front properties only, both villas and condos.

COZUMEL INSIDER PROPERTY RENTAL
www.cozumelinsider.com/proprentals
011-52-987-869-0504

A small selection of villas and condos. Call Sherri Davis, she sometimes has properties not listed on the site yet.

COZUMEL VACATION RENTALS
www.islacozumel.net/homes
1-713-523-1013

Rentals from $495 weekly to $7,790
In town and beach areas.

COZUMEL VACATION VILLAS
www.cozumel-villas.com
1-800-224-5551

Wide assortment of ocean front, beach, and in-town properties.

TRAVEL NOTES VILLA RENTAL
www.travelnotes.cc
1-800-266-5639

Rentals from $450 for a 3 bedroom, no pool to $7350 for a 10 bedroom beach front with pool, and everything in between. I have personally used this company, and they were very helpful.

OTHER VILLA RENTAL WEB SITES:

www.cozumel-vacation-rental-homes.com

www.idealvacationrentals.com

www.ivponline.com

www.mexonline.com

Www.realadventures.com

www.rent101.com

www.rentalscozumel.com

www.vacationhomes.com

Note: The same villas will be offered on several sites, check around for the best deal on a particular villa. It is also sometimes better if you lease through the company that actually does the property management in Cozumel for that property.

A SAMPLE LISTING OF VILLAS AND CONDOS

CASA BONITA In town property. 3 bedroom/3 bath, AC, Cable TV, sleeps 6, no pool. $450–$650

CASA MARCOS In town. 3bedroom/1family room, 2 ½ bath, AC, Cable TV, Phone, BBQ, Pool/patio/palapa. Sleeps 10-11. $975–$1200

Casa Marcos pool area.

PUESTA del SOL CONDOS Water front north. 3 bedroom, 2 bath, AC, Satellite TV, VCR, Internet access, Pool, phone. $1190–$1400

VILLA RANAS SUR Ocean front south. 10 bedroom, 10 bath, beach, phone, TV, private pier. $7350–$8750

CASA CASADA In town. 3 bedroom, 3 bath, cable TV,5 terraces, AC, pool with waterfall. $1550–$1700
Sleeps 6-8

ISLAMAR VACATION VILLAS In town. 1 and 2 bedroom condos, 1or 2 baths, TV, phone, BBQ, pool, Jacuzzi, gear tank and lockers sleep 2-4 $$385–$875

This is only a very small sample of what is available on the Isle. It is best to check the websites I have listed, get on the discussion boards and ask for reviews from others who have stayed at a property you are interested in. Renting your own place, whether a studio apartment, or the largest villa on the island, is a wonderful experience.

CHAPTER IV

GETTING AROUND COZUMEL

Auto-Bus-Taxi-Bike

GETTING AROUND COZUMEL

Depending on where you are staying and what plan to do, there are several options for getting where you want to go. If you are staying down town, a rental car is not necessary on a daily basis, although you may want to rent for one or two days, in order to visit the East side beaches and ruins.

You can walk to many of the best restaurants, shopping, dive piers, even the museum. For places a little to far for your stamina, taxi fares are very reasonable. (see list of fares) There is also a new bus service that was recently added, it will take you from town to the north and south end beaches and hotels. The cost is 10 to 20 pesos, or $1–$2.

Bicycles are another fun option and are especially great for exploring the local neighborhoods and finding those hidden little shops and restaurants. Bikes can be rented by the day or week, or bring your own if you are staying awhile. Better yet, buy one and give it to a child when you leave.

Scooters are available from several car rental operations at an average cost of $25 per day. This is the one form of transportation we do not recommend. There are and have been frequent injuries and fatalities to both locals and tourists. If you rent a car, please watch for the mopeds, they are sometimes hard to spot. If you have a MC license, you can rent a full size bike from Big Boys Bikes, the only place these are available. Contact Tony Rome at the Embassy Restaurant.

Car rentals are available from many places at many different prices. Both major chains such as Avis and National are there, and there are several good local choices as well. Shop on the internet, send emails and bargain during slow season. Be clear what your agreed upon price includes, some will include insurance, for others it is additional. Speaking of insurance, unless you have A LOT of cash or available credit, take the extra insurance. If you have an accident in Mexico, whether it is your fault or not, if there are damages, you could land up in jail, or not allowed to leave until fault has been decided and payment made.

Rental vehicle range from the topless VW bug to a full size van. Be sure to check and document prior damages before accepting the vehicle. Also be aware that parking is limited, best to use the parking lots that charge a few pesos and walk around. If you park on a red curb you may be towed, or your plates removed, and you will have to pay to get the car or the plates back.

When driving in Cozumel avenidas have the right of way. Calles stop at every corner except where there is two way traffic. The green light on the stop light flashes when it is getting ready to change. Juarez separates the town into North and South. Even numbered calles are on the North side and odd numbered calles are on the South side. Right turns are usually permitted at a red light.

CAR RENTALS

Popular Island Rental

ALAMO 1-800-462-5266 www.alamo.com
Maritime terminal
Puerto Maya
Downtown

AVIS 1-800-331-1084 www.avis.com
Airport 011-52-987-872-0219
Downtown 011-52-987-872-1923 ½ block off plaza
Fiesta Americana 011-52-987-872-9600
Maritime terminal 011 52-987-872-0094

BUDGET   1-800-472-3325   www.budget.com
Airport
Downtown Ave 5 between Calle 2 & 4

HERTZ   1-800-654-3030   www.hertz.com
Downtown Ave 15 & Calle 10
Puerto Maya Pier
Punta Langosta
Maritime terminal

LESS PAY   1-888-829-8084   www.islacozumel.net/services/lesspay
Downtown #628 Melger Ave @ Barracuda Hotel 011-52-987-872-4744
Park Royal Hotel

MARLIN   011-52-987-872-5501   www.gocozumel.com/marlin
Downtown Ave 10 between Calle 2 & Juarez

NATIONAL   1-800-227-3876   www.nationalcar.com
Downtown

RENTADORA AGUILA/WALKER 1-800-224-5551   www.cozumelcars.com
Info@cVvmexico.com
#685 Melger Ave between Calle 3&5
Ask for Ricardo, he will often give you a deal in slow season.

RENTADORA ISIS 011-52-987-872-3367   www.islacozumel.net/services/isis
Downtown Ave 5 between Calle 2&4

SMART CAR   011-52-987-872-5651   www.gocozumel.com/smartcar
Across from Airport Ave 65
Downtown Calle 1 & Ave 10
Across from Puerto Maya Pier @ Pemex station

THRIFTY   1-800-847-4389   www.thrifty.com
Airport
Downtown

BIG BOYS BIKES   011-52-987-872-0131

TONYROME@PRODIGY.NET.MX

Ave 5 between Salas & Calle 3 @ Tony Rome's Embassy Restaurant

Note: If you receive a good deal arranged on the internet, please bring copy of your confirmation or email, as sometimes the local agent will say they do not have such a rate. If you have the paper confirming they will not argue.

BICYCLE RENTALS

ISLA BICYLETA   011-52-987-878-4919

www.gocozumel.com/cozumelbikerentals

Ave 10 between Salas & Calle 1   cozumelbikes@gocozumel.com

They rent road bikes, mountain bikes, and old fashioned comfort bikes. Unfortunately, adult tricycles are not available on the island. Included with rental are helmet, gloves, locks, pumps, and tire gauge.

$7.00 ½ day $13.00 full day $58 weekly   Bike tours Available also rents snorkel gear $5.00.

RENTADORA ISIS   011-52-987-872-3367

www.islacozumel.net/services/isis

Downtown Ave 5 between Calle 2&4   cozumelricardo@aol.com

$10.00 full day $49.00 weekly

Note: Many of the hotels, vacation villas, and B&Bs offer free use of bikes to their rentals. Inquire about this when making your reservations.

TAXI FARES

All fares are approximate due to the fluctuation in the exchange rates. Be sure to agree on the fare before getting in, or ask driver to see the fare schedule. Try to have the correct change or close to it, as some drivers will tell you they can not make change.

From Punta Langousta Pier:

Down town	$4	El Presidente Hotel	$7	Mercado	$5
Palmar Estate	$5	Fiesta Americana	$8	Chakanaab Park	$10
Playa corona	$10	Cozumel Country Club	$10	Chen Rio Beach	$21
San Clemente Beach	$13	MR Sanchos	$15	Playa Bonita	$24
San Francisco beach	$13	Nachui Cocom	$15	Punta Sur	$30
North Hotel Zone	$8	Palancar Beach	$20	San Gervasio	$45 rt
Playa Azul	$8	Punta Morena	$19	Paradise Beach	$13
Puerto de Abrigo	$6	El Cozumeleno	$8	Ranch Las Palmas	$15
Melia	$8	Club del Sol	$7	Air port	$9
Puerta Maya Pier	$6	Playa Mia Beach	$15	Punta Francesa	$18

From Puerta Maya Area:

El Presidente Hotel	$6	Mercado	$6		
Palmar Estate	$7	Fiesta Americana	$7	Chakanaab Park	$10
Playa corona	$10	Cozumel Country Club	$15	Chen Rio Beach	$25
San Clemente Beach	$12	Mr. Sanchos	$14	Playa Bonita	$30
San Francisco beach	$12	Nachui Com	$14	Punta Sur	$30
North Hotel Zone	$12	Palancar Beach	$17	San Gervasio RT	$45
Playa Azul	$12	Punta Morena	$25	Paradise Beach	$13
El Cozumeleno	$8	Ranch Las Palmas	$5	Melia	$12
Airport	$12	Playa Mia Beach	$14		

From Downtown:

Within downtown	$2	El Presidente Hotel	$6	Mercado	$2
Cozumel Palace	$4	Fiesta Americana	$6	Chakanaab Park	$9
Playa Corona	$11	Cozumel Country Club	$5	Chen Rio Beach	$15
San Clemente Beach	$14	Mr. Sanchos	$13	Allegro	$17
San Francisco Beach	$14	Nachui Com	$13	Playa Bonita	$18
North Hotel Zone	$5	Palancar Beach	$20	San Gervasio	$45rt

Playa Azul	$5	Punta Morena	$13	Paradise Beach	$11
Reef club	$12	Casa Del Mar	$4	Ranch Las Palmas	$8
Melia	$5	Puerta Maya Pier	$6	Playa Mia Beach	$13
Oberstar	$17				

Taxis anywhere off the main drag to anywhere back in town is $15 pesos. A taxi that is flying a red flag is working in town and not on Melgar. They switch days so everyone gets to work Melgar. Taxis with no numbers have had their license taken away from them and will not stop for you.

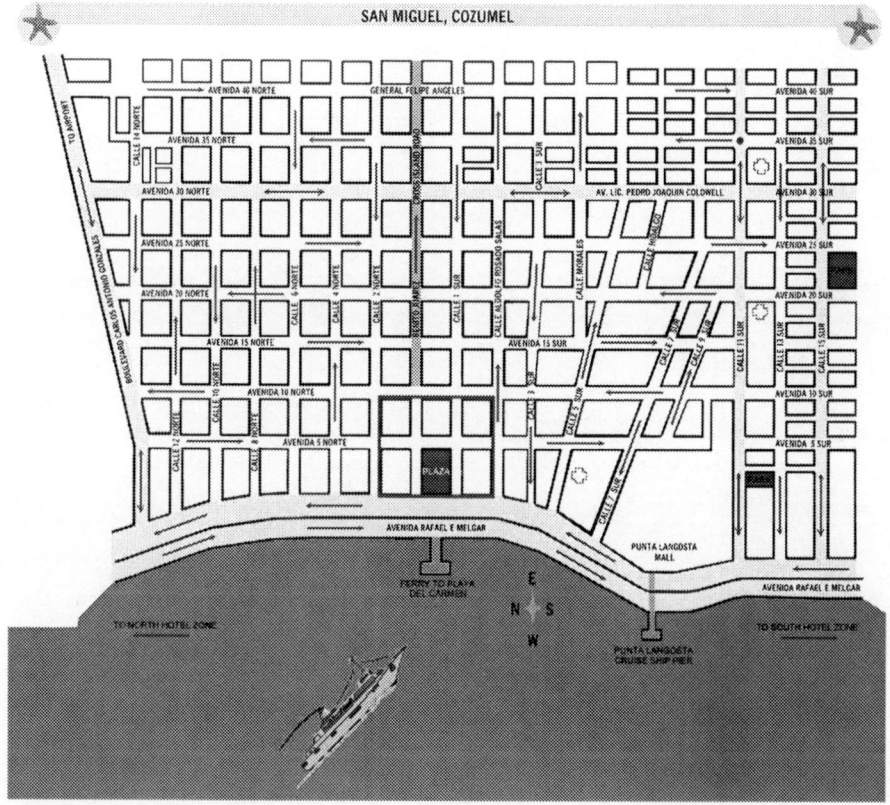

Map Courtesy of Stephen Young

CHAPTER V

DINING IN COZUMEL

EAT FOR $2.00 OR $100.00

DINING IN COZUMEL

The wide array of dining choices is amazing for such a small island with only one town. There is so much to choose from, everyone can be satisfied from the pickiest child to the gourmet snob. There are close to one hundred dining establishments on Cozumel, but I have only listed those that I have either had experience with, or someone I know has patronized. I also am listing a few of the chain restaurants without reviews, after all, what more can be said about Pizza Hut or McDonalds.

To really savor the true taste of the Mayan Yucatan you most dine at a few of the small local Taquerias and Cocina Economicas (lunch on the run), it is at these small establishments that you will get a real sample of how the locals eat. The ethnicity of the food on the island is very diverse, Mexican, Mayan, American, Asian Argentinean, French, and more. If you are looking for something particular, just ask on one of the discussion boards, someone will know.

Restaurants open and close here every year, but the majority have been around for some time. Many times a new establishment is only a new name, as often a chef or partner will venture out on his own to open a business, after cooking elsewhere for years. If you come across a restaurant that is not listed in this book, by all means please try it out and then let us know about it.

Please be aware that sometimes a taxi driver will tell you that a restaurant is closed or no longer exists. This is usually a ploy to direct you to another dining establishment where he will then get a bonus for delivering you to them. If this should happen to you, insist that you be taken to that address or get out and use another taxi.

Bon Appetite!!

ECONOMICAL

ASADERO EL POLLO
30th Ave between Morelos & Calle 5

They close when they run out of chicken…it can be as early as 3pm or as late as 7pm. Prices are inexpensive at 60 pesos. The grilled chicken is really yummy, and it comes with bags of rice, salsa, onions, and lots of corn tortillas.

CAFÉ SAN AGUSTIN
Calle 10 & Ave 15
NO CC

Delicious breakfasts and desserts. Serves gourmet coffees and teas.

CAMILLO'S
Ave 5 & Calle 2
NO CC

This inexpensive seafood restaurant serves up the yummiest fried shrimp tacos at only 10 pesos each. This is open air dining, a very popular locals place. No English is spoken, but the menu is very simple to order from, just point.

CAREYCITO'S
Ave 65 between Calles 2&4
NO CC open 7pm–11pm

A great place to stop in and have an evening snack of Salbutes (small tortillas with a variety of toppings), or some tasty Panuchos (tortillas filled with beans and topped with lettuce, tomatoes, onions, and meat)

CHILANGOS
Ave 30 between Calle 3 & Moralos
NO CC 6 pm–1am

You have only two choices to pick from here, both delicious. Quesadillas or huaraches (folded over tortillas). Choose your toppings and fillings from behind the glassed in case, just point as needed. A favorite here is the nopales which is cactus, very good, give it a try.

COCIINA MEDITERRANEAN
P Salas between Ave 5 & 10
NO CC 9am–7pm

This is a very new addition to the local dining scene. Owned and operated by a nice lady named Ruth, she is serving up some great omelets, tortas, and her Mediterranean specialties. Try the spinach and cheese pastries, hmmmm melt in your mouth good.

COCOS   872-0241
Ave 5 ½ block from Plaza
NO CC

Serving breakfast only, this is popular with the locals and expats, and myself, who sometimes are lined up in the morning waiting for opening time. Sit outside at a sidewalk table and people watch while you enjoy your morning coffee. Food is good and prices are reasonable.
Need a book to read on the beach, this is the place. Bring an old book and exchange or buy a used paperback for a dollar.

COFFEE PRESS
Calle 6 & Ave 5
NO CC

No English is spoken here, but not a problem ordering off the menu. Operating out of a cute little house which the owners have converted into a restaurant. Prices are very reasonable with an order of Eggs Benedict and coffee under $5.00 U.S.

COFFELIA'S
Calle 5 between Ave 5 & 10
NO CC

Excellent choice for a light lunch. Specialty is scrumptious Crepes filled with your choice of items.

EL CASINO
Ave 5 between Salas & Calle 3
NO CC

Serving Cuban specialties at very inexpensive prices. Good for an economy dinner.

EL MERCADO
Salas between Ave 20–25
NO CC

This is not just one eatery, but at least 5 small open air restaurants around the Mercado. They get crowded at breakfast with locals and visitors who know how to stretch their food budget. I have eaten breakfast at several of them and for under $3 U.S. I had very good and filling breakfasts.

EL MUSEO
Waterfront @ Museum
NO CC

Basic good food made even better by the setting and view. Sit out on the balcony overlooking the waterfront and enjoy the cool Caribbean breeze. Especially popular at breakfast.

EL PICA
Ave 30 & Juarez
NO CC opens at 7pm

A local taqueria serving Tacos Pasture and gringas, which are Tacos Pasture with added cheese. 5 or 6 of these at 5 pesos a piece plus a coke and you have dinner for under $3.50.

EL SITO TACOS   876-1558
Calle 2 between Melger & Ave 5
NO CC 7am-noon

Be adventures and eat breakfast like a local. Serving some of the best seafood tacos and sandwiches in town. If you can not accept eating this for breakfast then get them to go and take them on the boat or to the beach for your lunch.

EL TURIX   872-5234
Ave 20 between Calle 17 & 19
NO CC Dinner only

Located in a residential area serving Yucatecan dishes. A very simple establishment with excellent food and a friendly smiling staff. My favorite dishes here are the Panuchos (fried tortilla with chicken and avocado), and the chicken in black chili sauce.

GARDEN OF EATIN   011-52-987-878-4020
Calle Salas between Melger & Ave 5
NO CC

I would recommend this place as the #1 choice for vegetarians. Fantastic salads and vegetable dishes at excellent prices.

GRAND SLAM
Ave 30 across from Dominos
NO CC

A local torta eatery serving a torta special for $2.25 U.S.. It is a combination of pulled pork, ham, cheese, grilled onions, letchuga, and avocado on a French roll. Eat one of these and you are set until dinner time.

LA CANDELA
Ave 5 & Calle 6
NO CC

This place is jam packed with locals by mid afternoon. Serving home made Yucatan food worth far more than the $45 pesos they charge. For that price you get a choice of soup, choice of 3 entries, which change daily, rice or spaghetti, and veggies or potatoes. Also comes with a cold drink of Jamica (a tea made from hibiscus). Be sure to try the chicken cutlet stuffed with ham if it is available. They have recently started serving breakfasts.

LA COZUMELENA
Ave 10 & Calle 3
NO CC Breakfast/lunch

They have their own bakery on site for fresh bread and pastries. Serving both Mexican and American style breakfast. My large group of teens had no complaints and ate everything in sight.

LA MISSION
30th Avenue between Juarez and Calle 2
NO CC

Meat and pork chop tacos, frijoles charros, and salsa bar. I understand they are now serving breakfast for $20 pesos and up.

LA PERLITA   872-3452
Ave 65 between calle 8&10
MC, V Lunch only

Cerviche and fried fish are the main stays at this neighborhood restaurant and seafood market. Crowded with locals and families, definitely worth a taxi ride to sample their delicious fish.

LAS FLAMITAS
Ave 25 between Calle 3 & Morelos
NO CC

Another terrific Cocina Economica with a big bang for your Peso. No English spoken, but it is worth the effort to eat here. $3–$5 gets you soup, entrée, and drink, with a choice of 5–6 entrees daily. The Sopa de lima is highly recommended.

LAS SERAS TAQUERIA
Ave 30 & Morelos
NO CC Dinner til 1am

Some of the best tacos Al Pastor on the island.$4.5 pesos per taco. Two people can eat for $6–$7 U.S. including Cokes.

LONCHERIA LAS PALMAS
Ave 25 & Calle 3
NO CC Lunch/Dinner

A popular dining place for the locals. Daily specials include soup, entrée, and drink for $4.50 U.S.. A bit more expensive, but still cheap is the shrimp brochette, a grilled shrimp dish that is out standing.

LOS TRES GATITOS
Calle 7 between Ave 10 & 15
NO CC Opens @ 7pm

No English spoken here, but just point to the menu to order. Serving Mexican snacks and finger foods. Fill your tummy for under $3.00 U.S.

RILEY'S TAVERN   872-4001
A R Salas between Ave 10 & 15

Cozumel's only American style tavern. Serves Hamburgers, sandwiches and fries at decent prices.

ROTISERIA TRIUNFO
30th Ave & Calle 4

The rotisserie chicken is wonderful. Cooked by a natural wood fire it has a wonderful flavor and is very tender and juicy. Only available "to go", and a whole chicken were 60 pesos. They will cut up the chicken and it comes with tortillas, spaghetti noodles and sliced cabbage.

SABORES
Ave 5 between Calle 3 & Salas
NO CC

Another popular cocina economica with home style Yucatan cooking. For less than $5.00 us you get soup, entrée, rice, veggie, and drink. Eat in the dining room, or enjoy your meal in the garden.

SAN MIGUEL CAFÉ
Ave 15 between Calle 2 & 4
NO CC B, L, D

English is spoken here, so ordering is no problem. At breakfast and dinner order off their menu. At lunch they serve the specials of soup, entrée, veggie, and drink for under $5.00 U.S.. On Friday evenings there is live music.

SANTA CARLOS
Ave 50 between Calle 3 & 5
NO CC

A popular local seafood place. Located in the garden of a local fish market, they serve the freshest and best priced fish dinners on Cozumel Dinner for two, including 2 cervasas each is less than $160 pesos ($16 U.S.).
Look for the yellow sign that says Pescadura (fish market).

TONITAS
Rosada Salas between Ave 10 & 15
NO CC B, L

Typical home style Yucatan cooking. The Pazole (chicken soup) comes highly recommended by friends.

VIVA MEXICO
Ave Juarez between Calle 60 & 65 bis
NO CC

Terrific tacos and guacamole served here, but the real specialty is the Pazole made with pork or chicken and hominy.

MODERATE

ALL SPORTS BAR   869-2246
Ave 5 & Calle 2
10:am–1:30am

Good Mexican dishes, steaks, and seafood. Good place for a snack while watching your favorite teams on wide screen TV. You can also place bets on all the sports, and maybe win big!

AL FREDO di ROMA   872-0322
Hotel Presidente
V, MC, AX

Serving gourmet Italian and Mexican fare, this new addition is quickly becoming popular. A local owner and chef swears he will go broke from eating there so often.. Their pasta is reasonable, and I am told it is outstanding.

CASA BLANCA
Calle 1 on the plaza
No CC

A personal favorite of the author's fussy teens. A terrific place to people watch as it is right on the corner of the plaza. Serving many Yucatan specialties, but the nachos with chicken are really yummy and the serving is large. Don't forget to purchase the Casa Blanca souvenir, a painted tile with a Senor or Senorita and your name and Casa Blanca on it. Ask for Jose and tell him Patricia sent you.

CASA DENNIS
Calle 1 just off the plaza   872-0067
NO CC

This is the oldest restaurant on Cozumel and a long time favorite of locals and visitors alike. A great place for people watching on the plaza, or listening to the strolling musicians. It is another favorite of the author, with too many terrific dishes to choose a favorite. Serves B, L, D, and is open quite late.

CHEN RIO
East coast beach road
NO CC

One of the most popular beach front restaurants on the East side, mostly for the beach location. Food is so-so, flies are annoying at times, but a fun place and serves a strong Margarita.

COCONUTS
East side beach rd
NO CC

Worth the visit for the awesome view alone. Set high on a cliff with a view of the beach and crashing surf. Enjoy a lunch of quesadias and a cold cervasa, or try the coconut shrimp hmmmm yummy. Bring a tee shirt from your home town to add to the ceiling of the palapa roof. There is a small secluded cove just below, but be sure to check it ahead before taking children down.

CONCHITA del CARIBE
Ave 65 between call 21 & 23
NO CC

Serving some of the best seafood on the Island for reasonable prices. The cerviche and seafood soup are both great to start a meal with, then have the catch of the day.

COSTA BRAVA
Calle 7, around the corner from post office
MC, V, AE

I have never had a bad meal here, whether it was breakfast, lunch or dinner. I get the same report from other Cozumel frequent visitors. Breakfast for two including eggs, meat, beans, coffee runs $6–7 U.S.. The conch and the lobster also gets high marks as does the Mexican platter for two. Bring them your catch when you fish, for $2 U.S. they will cook it up and serve it with side dishes.

EL MORRO
Ave 75 between Calle 2 & 4   872-3029
MC. V

A long time favorite of divers and locals, it has been discovered by other tourists due to its excellent food, good prices, and frequent mention in guide books. It is a bit far from the center of town, but well worth the trip. Fresh seafood of all types, the seafood platter is huge and will feed two persons with average appetites. The giant Margaritas and Pina coladas are good, but beware driving afterwards. Kid friendly with video games in the back.

ESPECIAS   876-1558
Calle 5 & Ave 10
NO CC Dinner only

World cuisine served in an open air setting. A must visit while in Cozumel. Adrian is the owner and chef at this fantastic little place. He is a member of the Casa Dennis family and I think he was born cooking. Argentinean and Mexican dishes, his meals are of gourmet quality, how he serves these dishes at these low prices is a mystery. Everything is wonderful here, but try the empanadas and the crab fingers. Only five tables, so I recommend reservations, and during holidays and Carnaval, call before you even get on the plane.

ERNESTO'S FAJITA FACTORY   872-1154
Melger, oceanfront, just north of la Ceiba

This is your basic Tex-Mex, that said, it is terrific Tex-Mex. Serves some of the best shrimp nachos and fajitas I have ever eaten. Noisy and fun, beware of the tequila shooters.

FRENCH QUARTER   872-6321
Ave 5 between Salas & calle 3
V, MC, AE Dinner only

The Big Easy has arrived in Cozumel. Serving authentic New Orleans Cajun food. Specialty is the filet minion with red onion marmalade. The jambalaya and etoufee is also good. Dine inside, or on the balcony.

JEANNIES WAFFLE HOUSE
Melger & Calle 11
MC, V

Another favorite of divers for that early morning breakfast. Large Mexican and American breakfasts. Although I was not impressed, basically a Mexican IHOP, my picky teens were quite happy and ate everything, and gets good reviews else where.

JOHNNY BRAVO'S
Ave 15 between Calle 3 & Salas
NO CC Dinner only

The specialty here is the Arrachero beef, which is grilled and placed on tortillas and topped with sauces, onions, and cilantro. Have a cold cervasa and your meal is complete.

LA CHOZA   872-0958
Ave 10 & Salas
MC, V

Serving from early morning to late evening, this is an excellent choice for any meal. Serves breakfast at low prices, has good lunch specials that locals are aware of, but the tourists need to ask about. Food is delicious and service is friendly.

LA MORENA   879-1923
Ave 10 between Calle 3 & 5
L, D CC?

Excellent seafood and Mexican dishes, but the big draw here is the Mexican Coffee prepared at your table. Coffee, tequila, coconut ice cream, and cinnamon....YUMMY

MANATI   044-987-1000-787 CELL
Ave 10 & Calle 8
NO CC 2pm–11pm closed Sundays

Small dining establishment located in a cute little wooden frame house. Personal attention from owner and chef Leo. International foods, including pasta, fish and Mexican. Offers a divers special from 2pm–6pm

PALMERAS   872-0532
Melger in front of the ferry terminal
V, MC, AE B, L, D

Can you say Denny's in Spanish! But then I actually like Denny's. The food is pretty good and the fried fish I ate was extremely good. Get a street front table for breakfast and people watch as all the cruise ship tourists descend and the ferries unload. This is definitely the place for dinner during Carnaval, get there early and have a very long dinner, and a front seat for viewing the parades.

LAS TORTUGAS   872-1242
Pedro Joaquin Coldwell @ Calle 19
Dinner only CC?

The name translates to "The Turtles". This is a traditional Mexican restaurant, you will not find Tex-Mex here. Try the conch cerviche, I am told it is very good.

NINO'S PIZZA   2 LOCATIONS   989-6042/872-4166
Ave 10 & Calle 3
Ave 65 between calle 21 & 25
No CC

Open long hours and will deliver to your hotel or villa. I have only used the Ave 10 location, but it was the best Pizza I have tried so far in Cozumel. Since I often bring teen boys, I use them at least once or twice a trip. A large pizza was approximately $8.00 U.S.

ROCK'N JAVA
602 Melger
NO CC B, L

A long time favorite of locals and tourists alike. Serves a good breakfast and very good salads. A good choice of dining for vegetarians. If you want to donate to the Humane Society, or drop off supplies for them, this is the place to do it.

TONY ROME'S EMBASSY RESTAURANT   872-0131
Ave 5 between Salas & Calle 3
NO CC Opens @ 3pm

If you do not go to Tony's, you haven't been to Cozumel. Tony and his wife Maria Jose are your warm and friendly hosts for the evening. He has the BEST ribs in town, served with his own special sauce. No connection to the Tony Roma chain, but ask him to tell you that story, very interesting, and the ribs here are above and beyond any others I have had. The meat falls off and melts in your mouth. Other dishes are good too, but do not leave without a piece of either Key Lime pie, or Mango Pie. He will also cook your catch from that fishing charter.

Terrific place for groups and parties, there is a large raise dance floor, and Tony will entertain you. A former Las Vegas entertainer, he has the voice of an angel and can sing anything you request. If you are brave, get up and do the karaoke thing. Free phone call home with dinner, and free use of his internet to check/send email. Oh, and the reason it is called the Embassy, is that any information or help needed with a problem on the island, Tony is the guy who can help!

EXPENSIVE

AQUARIO   872-1097
Ocean front Melger @ calle 11
V, MC

Beachfront seating with beautiful sunsets, excellent service, and great food. Live jazz and candle light add to the romance. The orange shrimp is a well known favorite here.

AL CAPI NAVEGANTE   872-1730
312 Ave 10
V, MC, AE dinner only

Primarily a seafood restaurant, although there are two chicken and two steak choices for those who do not eat seafood. Servings are large and the food is good. Served in a very nice sea themed décor. Be sure to leave room for flambé desserts prepared at tableside.

AMBARS
5 Av #141 Between 1 and Rosado Salas   869-1955
Dinner only

Serving gourmet Italian fare in a romantic setting on the terrace. Nice place for that special date.

CASA MISSION   872-1641
Juarez & calle 55
V, MC, AE

The main attraction here are the beautiful gardens and mini zoo with monkey and lion on display. The fajitas seem to be the favorite item. Reviews of this establishment are mixed, so try it for yourself, if only for the attractions it offers.

LA LOBSTERIA
Ave 5 & Calle 7
NO CC dinner only

A fairly new addition to the dining scene is receiving good reviews and high marks from those who have eaten here. Fresh lobster. Fish, and shrimp served with fresh veggies and rice. Try a bowl of Sopa de Marccosas a seafood soup, they say there is enough seafood in it to call it a main entrée.

LA LOBSTERIA

LA VERANDA   872-4132
Calle 4 between Ave 5 & 10
MC, V

Most likely the most romantic setting for a restaurant on the island. Try the shrimp Caribbean prepared and flamed at your table, or seafood salad for two ($38 U.S.).

LA VERANDA

LOBSTER HOUSE
NORTH HOTEL ZONE
NO CC dinner only

Serves the biggest lobsters they can find. Pick your own dinner out from the tank. A long time favorite for lobster, nothing else is served here.

GUIDO'S   872-0946
#23 Avenida Rafael E. Meglar
V, MC

Best known for their gourmet pizzas which are baked in wood burning ovens and their famous sangria. Be sure to get an order of the garlic bread, quite different from what we are accustomed to, but tastes awesome. To get away from the heat of the ovens, dine out on the patio, it is more romantic anyway.

LA COCAY   872-5533
Calle 8 between Ave 10 & 15
V, MC L, D

Recently reopened at this new location, I have been assured that the menu and quality of the food remains as high as ever. This is perfect to celebrate that birthday or anniversary. Gourmet Mediterranean cuisine such as Tuna tartar with avocado wasabi mayonnaise for appetizer, and entrees such as almond and vanilla bean crusted fish of the day.

MESA 17   878-4928
Calle 17 & Ave 25
NO CC

Fine dining at its best, definitely world class. Trish and Glen are your wonderful hosts/owners and will make you feel at home, while treating you like royalty. An ever changing menu, "Comida del Mundo", or "food of the world". Their Thai red curry with shrimp is a must try as is the shrimp and pineapple soup. This is a perfect choice for a special evening. If you have a special wine you would like to bring, they will serve it for you at a small corkage fee.

MEXICO EN LOS SIGLOS   869-1797
Melger Ave 1 mi south of Plaza
V, MC L, D

Translating to "Mexico through the centuries", their menu consists of recipes from all of Mexico. The dining here is true gourmet Mexican. The quality and taste is excellent, but it is the presentation that stands out, meals look like works of art. The serving of Mahi Mahi was so large I had to share it with my companion.

PANCHO'S BACKYARD
Melger Ave @ Los Cinco Soles
V, MC, AE

Located within the Los Cinco Soles store, this is a popular establishment with tourists. Food is decent and service is excellent. A nice place to have an elegant lunch after shopping.

PEPE'S GRILL
Melger & Salas
MC, V, AE

Definitely not for the economy minded, but a nice choice for a special night out. Ocean view dining and good food in elegant surroundings. Serving steaks and seafood, but for dessert try the orange crepes with Spanish coffee.

PRIMA'S   872-6567
Salas & Ave 5
V, MC, AE Dinner only

Italian pasta dishes, seafood, and the freshest salads in Cozumel. This establishment is upstairs on a second floor with a large veranda to dine on. Enjoy people watching while you eat. A very busy and popular place, you may have to wait for a table.

IF YOU MUST!!!

BURGER KING 3 locations: Ferry pier
                                     Punta Langosta mall
                                     Chedraui Mall

DOMINO'S PIZZA	Calle 5	delivers	872-1635
HARD ROCK CAFÉ	Melger between Calle 7 & 11		872-5271
KFC	Melger waterfront		872-0310
MCDONALDS	Melger waterfront		881-7700

| PIZZA HUT | Melger & Calle 5 | delivers | 872-5055/5056/5057 |
| SUBWAY | Melger & Calle 5 | | 872-3678 |

DINING AT YOUR VILLA

If you have rented a casa or villa and have cooking facilities, you can save some vacation dollars and have some fun at the same time. Shop in the Mercado or the local grocery stores for food and supplies. Take some lessons in Spanish cooking or just use a few of the recipes listed at the end. The Fruit, veggies, meat and fish on the island are fresh and will taste so good. When ever I bring a group, we always have a pool side dinner party or BBQ at least once or twice…really a lot of fun and stretches the budget.

SHOPPING FOR FOOD

Mercado: Ave 25 & Salas
The freshest fruit and veggies in town at the lowest prices. Meats, poultry and fish also available, although it is hung in the open and it will depend how you feel about this.

Cedraui's:
At edge of town, near Melger and Calle 11.
A Mexican version of a super Wal-mart, stocking groceries, meats, produce, and of course all the non food items. Also has beer and some liquors at decent prices, and a deli section.

Local Modern Super Market

San Francisco Markets: 2 locations: Ave 30 & Juarez/Ave 65 & Calle 23
Mexican supermarket, compares with American small Winn Dixie. Deli in store.

Super Maz: Ave 30 & Calle 8
Another nice supermarket, sometimes has things not available in the others.

Sedena's: Melger and Airport Blv
This is a small market, but often has something not found it the others. Has the best price on Vanilla in town. Prices are good here.

Pacadeli: Ave 45 & Calle 2
A small shop that carries a lot of imports and items normally unavailable in Cozumel

Shopping tip
Remember when ordering by weight that 1 kilogram is equal to 2.2 pounds.

COOKING LESSONS

ISLAND CUISINE COOKING CLASSES

You can have your choice of a demonstration class or hands on. Either the school will choose a dish, or you can make a special request when you reserve. You will receive a souvenir picture of class, an apron and a sample spice packet, included in the pricing Each class is 3–4 hrs.

Prices range from $42 us–$65 us including all materials.

www.cozumelinsider.com/cooking for reservations.

SAMPLE RECIPES FROM MEXICO

Tortilla soup

Ingredients:

3 tablespoons olive oil
4 corn tortillas, torn into spoon-sized pieces
5 garlic cloves, minced
1 large onion, puréed
3 large, ripe tomatoes, puréed
1 jalapeno pepper
1 can green chili's, diced
1 can tomato sauce
8 cups chicken stock
salt, pepper and chili powder to taste
1 large can chunk chicken

Garnishes:
1 cup shredded cheddar cheese
crispy tortilla chips, cut into strips.

The onion and tomato may be puréed together in your blender or food processor.

Heat the olive oil in a large soup pot. Sauté the tortilla pieces with the garlic until tortillas soften. Add the puréed onion, tomato and jalapeno pepper and simmer for 15 minutes. Add the canned tomato sauce, green chili's, chicken stock and chunk chicken. Bring to a boil, then reduce heat, cover and simmer for 30 minutes. Check seasonings, and add salt, pepper and chili powder as desired.
Serve hot, and garnish each serving with cheddar cheese and crisp tortilla strips.

SHRIMP DIABL0

Ingredients

1 lb. jumbo shrimp
1–1/2 cups water
½ stick of butter
1 medium onion chopped
4 cloves of fresh garlic, diced
3 chilies Serrano
4 large tomatoes
¼ cup of tomato paste
2 tablespoons lime juice
Salt and fresh ground black pepper
Cilantro (if desired)
Two chilies guajillo *red pepper

Clean and de-vein shrimps. Allow to sit in the refrigerator for 30 minutes.

Cook the tomato on open gas flame or electric burner (can be done in heavy skillet) until the skins break open. You can remove the skin, but I don't. Cut the tomato into wedges and put into a blender. Add chili guajillo. (Also the chili serranos if you want this HOT, leave out if you want this hot.). Add water, lime juice and blend into a sauce along with the tomato paste.

In a skillet, sauté the onion and garlic in the butter until the onion is clear and add the shrimp and sauté on high heat until the shrimp are very pink. Remove shrimp and hold in a bowl until later.

Add the sauce you've made in the blender to the skillet with the onion and garlic. Simmer this mixture for 20 to 30 minutes allowing the flavors to marry Return the shrimp to the sauce and simmer another 20 minutes. Add salt and pepper.

Serve this over steamed rice and adorn with finely chopped cilantro, if desired. Cut lemon into wedges and serve along side.

Salsa Jardinera
2 Spinach leaves washed
1/4 cup Yogurt natural
Salt and Pepper to taste
1/2 onion sliced very thin
2 tablespoons of butter

Cut the spinach in strips and sauté with the onion in butter, remove from fire, add the yogurt and serve immediately

Salsa Poblana
4 green ancho chilies
1/4 cup of cream
salt and pepper to taste
100 grams fresh cheese

Grill the chilies to break and peal the skin and remove seeds. Add to warmed cream with salt and pepper, the heat a little. Serve adorned with the fresh cheese.

Three Cheese Sauce
100 grams. Manchego cheese
100 grams. Gruyere cheese
100 grams. Parmesan Cheese
1/4 cup medium to heavy cream

Melt the cheeses with the cream to form a sauce and pour over baked chicken breast or vegetables. Serve hot.

Bistek Mexicana

This is a traditional Mexican dish that's very easy to make and excellent accompanied with refried beans, guacamole salad and/or Spanish rice.

Bisteak is sliced beef from a roast cut. Mexicans don't normally prepare roast beef, so this is one of the things that happen to that cut of meat.

Use about 2 pounds to feed six persons. Have it sliced in pieces about 1/8" to ¼" thickness.

2 Lbs Bisteak as above
10 Chilies Serrano, cut up
2 Medium onions, sliced 1/4" thick
3 Tomatoes, sliced in wedges
1 Cup of beef bullion
1/2 cup chopped cilantro

In a large heavy pot (I use a pressure cooker), put a small amount of cooking oil and heat hot. Quick fry the individual slices of meat about 50% done, until it is no longer red and remove from oil.

Add the bullion, return the meat, cover with the onion, chilies, and tomato wedges, cover and bring to a boil. Reduce heat to simmer and keep covered while cooking one hour or more until that beef is tender to cut with a fork. Serve adorned with cilantro with the veggies and tortillas.

I like to heat tortillas on open frame but can do it on an electric burner also. I put them directly on the flame/burner and turn them frequently until they are heated well.

Shrimp Enchiladas Corona

12 large shrimp
2 Corona Beers
4 Tablespoons of butter
1 Tablespoon of olive oil
6 Chiles de arbol (cayenne)
4 Tablespoons of chopped onion
4 Tablespoons of chopped enchalotes
1/4 Heavy cream
3 Tablespoons of Worcestershire sauce
1 Tablespoon of salt
1 Tablespoon of pepper

Clean the shrimp and marinate in half the beer with some of the salt and pepper for at least one hour.

Sauté the onion and enchalotes in butter and olive oil, until they are clear, add the shrimp and sauté until they turn pink. Add the Worcestershire, salt and pepper.

Cut the chilies in halves and add with the cream, heat and stir.

Take the shrimp out and set apart. Add the remaining beer to the salsa and reduce heat to simmer for 15 minutes. While it is simmering, relax and drink the other Corona. Place the sauce in a serving plate add the shrimp on top, adorn with the chilies.

If you cannot find enchalotes, omit from the recipe

FRUIT DRINK

3 cups of cubed fresh melon (cantaloupe, honeydew, or watermelon)
4 tablespoons of sugar
3 tablespoons of lime juice, fresh preferred

1 quart of water
Melon sliced for garnish

Place all in a blender and garnish. refreshing and tasty!

MEXICAN FOOD DEFINITIONS

Ancho Chile (AHN-choh)
    The dried version of the popular POBLANO chile. It is about 3–4 inches long and a dark, reddish brown. It is the sweetest of all the dried chile's with a slightly fruity flavor. Used in making sauces.

Arroz(AH-roz)
    Rice, usually referring to the long-grain, white variety

Barbacoa (bar-bu-KO-uh)
    Mexican 'pot roast' made from the cows head. Seasoned and baked with steam for hours until it is peel apart tender.

Bolillo(bo-EE-yo)
    Mexican ROLLS, usually about 6 inches in length.

Borracho (bo-ROTCH-o)
    Made with beer, usually referring to cooked PINTO beans, that are served like a soup.

Bunuelos (bun-WAY-los)
    Fried tortilla-like pastries that are a favorite during the holiday season. They are traditionally sprinkled with cinnamon sugar and served with a scoop of ice cream.

Burrito (burr-EE-toe)
    A large (10") flour tortilla filled with any number of concoctions including beans, beef, pork-then sealed by tucking the ends under. They can be eaten like this or topped with salsa, lettuce, tomato, cheese, or guacamole.

Carne (CAR-nay)
   Spanish and Mexican for meat, CARNE refers specifically to beef

Carne Asada—charcoal grilled pork or beef

Carne Guisada (CAR-nay GEE-sah-dah)
   Stewed meat made with beef, onions, bell peppers, garlic, salt, pepper, comino
   that is then served over white rice, or with Spanish rice and refried beans.

Ceviche—fish, shrimp, conch marinated with limon, vinegar, onions, tomatoes
and cilantro.

Chuleta Yucateca—Pork chop marinated in red adobado then grilled and
smothered with sautéed onions

Cilantro—the spice known in the USA as coriander

Cochinita Pibil—pork marinated in a sauce of achiote, natural orange juice and
spices, wrapped in fresh banana leaves, and slowly steamed.

Chorizo (CHORE-ee-so)
   Mexican Sausage, made with ground pork and spicy seasonings. In Mexico,
   fresh pork is used

Flan (flan)
   A dessert that closest resembles a caramel custard.

Flauta (FLOU-ta)
   Translates literally to "flute". This is a corn tortilla, usually white or yellow,
   that has been stuffed with beef, chicken, pork, or even beans-then rolled and
   pinned, then deep-fried until crisp.

Frijole con Puerco—A delicious local dish consisting of soupy black beans
cooked with chunks of pork. It's served with chopped radish, avacado, onion and
cilantro as garnish and steamed rice.

Guacamole (WOK-uh-mole-ee)
Avocado mixture that is made from ripened avocado's and lemon or lime juice, diced onion and tomato, cilantro. Guacamole is made by mixing by hand with a fork until the consistency still has very small (1/8") chunks of avocado. Never use a food processor for making guacamole!!

Horchata—a cold soft drink made of rice or barley, almonds, sugar, vanilla and water

Huevos (WAY-vose)
Eggs.

Huachinango—red snapper—usually served whole

Jalapeno (hall-a-PEN-yo)
A pepper that turns from green to red at maturity, these average about 2 inches in length. The 'hot' comes from the seed and membrane.

Jamaica—(ha-MY-ka) a delicious soft drink made from brewed hibiscus petals.

Masa (MAH-sah)
The Spanish word for "dough", masa is the corn flour dough used in making corn tortillas, tamales and gorditas. Dried corn is cooked in lime water, cooled, and then ground into masa.

Mero—fresh grouper usually served filet style

Mojo de Ajo—fish, coch or shrimp served in butter and garlic sauce

Mole—chicken or turkey meat or enchiladas baked in a thick spicy brown sauce made of almonds, chocolate chipotle peppers and peanut oil

Pan Dulce (pon-DUEL-say)
Pan Dulce are dome-shaped Mexican sweet rolls that are distinctive by the "shell" design on top. Most have a sugar topping with chocolate, lemon and vanilla being favorites

Platano Frito—tasty fried bananas

Pollo (PO-yo)
  Chicken.

Queso (k-SO)
  Cheese. In Mexico, goat's cheese is used for traditional dishes.

Queso "Gallo"—a Holland cheese, the same as Gouda, that has been imported to the Yucatan for so many years that it is now considered indigenous to the area

Queso Relleno—seasoned, ground pork/beef formed into a round "loaf", completely surrounded in softened

Queso Gallo and then wrapped in cheesecloth for cooking. Served in round slices covered in cream sauce.

Ranchero (ran-CHAIR-o)
  With tomatoes, bell peppers, garlic and onions as the backdrop, the word RANCHERO is used to describe either a salsa (cooked) or how something is cooked.

Salsa (SAL-sa)
  Sauce, refers generally to a tomato based condiment used to dip or to accent dishes.

Serrano Chile (seh-RAH-noh)
  A small (1 1/2 inches) fresh HOT pepper. As it matures, it will turn red, then yellow. A general rule with chile's is that the smaller they are in size, the more kick they have. The serrano chile is almost always used when making "pico de gallo"

Taco (tah-KOH)
  A Mexican or Tex-Mex sandwich eaten as an entree or snack. They are made with soft corn tortillas, fried corn tortillas folded over, or with hot, flour tortillas.

Tamales—chicken wrapped in a heavy dough and cooked in banana leaves

Tomatillo (TOM-a-tea-yo)
A small green Mexican fruit that is part of the tomato family. They are tough to the touch and are covered with a brown husk. Used mainly in making sauces, either fresh (fresca) or after simmering and then putting in a food processor with spices. This is the sauce used when the word VERDE (green) is used, i.e.: Enchiladas Verde.

Torta (TORE-tah)
Mexican "sub" sandwich that is made on a bolillo". (white or wheat roll)

Tortilla (tore-TEE-yu)
I is a round, thin "bread" made of either corn flour or wheat flour. Tortillas are cooked quickly on a hot COMAL and are eaten by themselves or can be used to wrap around anything imaginable and eaten as a TACO.

CHAPTER VI

SHOP–SHOP–SHOP

Tee shirts to diamonds, you can find it in Cozumel.

A local shop.

LET'S SHOP, SHOP, SHOP

Handicrafts, souvenirs, tee shirts, pottery, jewelry, liquor, clothing, it is all available in Cozumel. The best bargain in jewelry is the silver. Be sure to purchase in stores and check for the .925 mark to assure you are getting real sterling and not nickel silver. For gem stones and gold you can do as good or better at home. I have purchased gold there but only for some of the unique designs and not any super bargain on price. Black coral is an exception, but be sure to buy from a licensed dealer.

Good buys can be found on Yucatecan hammocks, leather goods, embroidered and lace clothing and table linens, silver jewelry, ceramics and decorative metalwork and carved wood.. You will also find high-quality handicrafts from all over Mexico—but because of the cost of importation to the island, you may find slightly better buys on these on the Mainland

Designer clothing is not a bargain here, but there are a few local stores that have designs you may not find at home, mostly sized for smaller women. Everyday clothing and beach wear is available at good prices. I often arrive with only an overnight bag for my self, dedicating the rest of my luggage to my charities, so I usually purchase what I need while there.

For small souvenirs such as ash trays, cups and glasses try the Chedrauis store, better prices than in the tourist areas. Liquor can also be a bargain in this store and other local liquor stores. Be sure to get a bottle of Rum Pope a local liqueur great in coffee.

Electronics are not cheap in Mexico, so be sure to bring your CD player, cameras and film. I found this out when I paid at least 4 times the value to replace my son's portable CD player.

A brief listing of some of my favorite shops is included in this book, but just because a shop is not listed, does not mean you should not shop there. If you find a favorite not listed, please let us know. Have fun bargaining where you can, but please remember these fine people have to make a living, so do not expect them to give their merchandise away. Bargaining is more likely in the smaller shops and where the prices are not clearly marked.

SHOPPING AREAS

PLAZA AND WATERFRONT AREA

The downtown and main square is a beautiful area with numerous shops selling Mexican and Mayan handicrafts and souvenirs. Jewelry shop after jewelry shop.

PUNTA LANGUSTA MALL

New mall area mostly with expensive up scale shops located at the downtown cruise pier.

PUERTO MAYA CRAFT MARKET

Crafts market close to where the cruise-ships dock, has crafts at good prices and convenient to all the ships in port. Across the Street from El Cid La Ceiba Hotel.

PUERTO MAYA MALL

A new shopping area with many of the same stores that are located downtown and a few new ones. A nice place to stroll around and shop. Close to the Puerto Maya cruise pier.

STORES

ALEGRIA INFANTIL

Ave 5.
A unique selection of kid's toys and games.

ArtePaz

Behind the Museum on Calle 6 between the waterfront and Avenida 5

Wholesaler of inexpensive beaded jewelry and enamel rings. You can bargain with the owner and get some really good deals.

Bien Raices
Melgar & Calle 8.

All kinds of interesting, handcrafted objects, and you can bargain. Lots of things not found in other shops.

Bikinis do Brasil
Calle 1 between Melger and Ave 5

Brazilian swimwear and sundresses. My size one 27-year old daughter can't miss this place every trip!

Bugamillias
Avenida 10 between Salas and Calle 1

Specializing in handmade lace and embroidered and woven table linens and clothing. Beautiful clothing and linens of high quality.

The Candy Store
Calle 2 between Avenida 5 and Avenida 10

Go there for the chocolate, it's heavenly.

Casa Bella
Calle 3 between Avenida 5 and 10.

Moderately-priced and beautiful decorative items including silver trays, pottery, lamps and more.

Chedraui
Near Ave 11 and Melger

This is a large store that is a combination of Wal-Mart and supermarket. Bigger than the San Francisco store, and slightly better prices. It's a good place to stock up at the beginning of your stay. They take credit cards!
Food, clothing and cheap souvenirs.

Cinco Soles
Melgar & Calle 8.

A large store with crafts from all over Mexico, nice jewelry, boutique section in the rear, and a 50% discount area. If you only have time for one store, this would be the one. Prices are set and no bargaining. Prices are fair, but if you have time, you might find lower prices several streets back off the square.

Covi Liquors
Avenida 30 and Calle 2

This is one of the best places to buy your tequila, rum, kaluha, etc. This is where many of the locals shop. It is far away from the tourist shops in town so the prices are WAY lower. For example, the prices for my favorite tequilas are literally half what they cost at Cinco Soles

CRAFTS MARKET
South side of the plaza at Calle 1

Has a good selection of crafts from Cozumel and other parts of Mexico.

Pottery shop

El Sombrero
Av. Rafael Melgar 29

Stocks leather clothing and accessories. Good prices if you bargain, and it smells so good in there.

Galeria Azul
Avenida 10 between Salas and Calle 1.

Original art of many talented Mexican artists can be found here.

Galleria Alexander
Av. 5 # 141

Galleria Alexander carries ceramics and paper Mache works created by the Mexican artist Alexander Flores.

Hammock Shop
Avenida 5 across the street from Zermatt's Bakery

Excellent buys from this Spanish man, but it helps if you speak some Spanish. He makes them himself

Havana Club Cigar Bar
Melger and Calle 8.

This is your best place for variety, quality and price on individual cigars as well as boxes

Cigar store sign

Instrumentales Musicales
Juarez and Avenida 20
Musical instruments from all over Mexico. If you're a musician-this is a must see for your list for the many antique instruments they have on display in his store.

L'Chic
Ave 5 and Calle 3.

Unusual clothes in styles you won't see in the US. Teens seem to like this store. Sizes are mostly small.

LA Concha
5 Ave one half block from the Plaza.
Gifts, folk art and weavings.

Mayan Feather
Av. 5 and Calle 2

Mayan Feather has original paintings on feathers from birds of the area. Prices are reasonable and many of the pictures are quite beautiful.

Mmro
Av. Rafael Melgar, near the town pier

Mexican resort wear with the latest designs and styles.

Miguelon y Hijos
Calle 5 and Avenida 15

This artist specializes in finely carved shell work that, is very cameo-esque in style. His work is often on display at the museum but you can go right to his workshop where he has other pieces displayed.

Muebles de la Santa Cruz
Avenida 15 between Calle 2 and Juarez.

Furniture and accessories in the wrought iron and carved wood rustic style. there are lots of small things to choose including talevera, wood and wrought iron lamps, picture frames, etc. Prices are very reasonable and well below what you would pay in the states.

Na Balam
Avenedia 5 # 14.

Specializes in Mayan artifact reproductions, textiles and fine jewelry.

Pipo Liquors
Avenida 30 and Calle 6

This is another good place to buy your tequila, rum, kaluha, etc. The prices are similar to COVI (check both places for your favorite items). Pipo has many brands that COVI doesn't carry.

Poco Loco
Av. Benito Juarez 2-A

Sells casual wear and beach bags

Roberto's Black Coral
5th Ave. and Calle A. Rosado Salas

Black coral can be made into jewelry and sculptures. Roberto's Black Coral is owned and operated by Roberto himself and his creations are top quality and made with REAL black coral. You must have a special license to sell black coral, and Roberto is one of the few who is legal.

The Talevera Store
Calle 1 between Avenida 20 and 25

Large selection of hand-painted Mexican pottery and a lot of really beautiful authentically hand-painted Talevera style pottery. Prices are a lot better than you'll see for similar items in the gift shops, and way less than some of the similar items I have seen in the import stores in the states.

Talavera
Av. 5 # 349

Not the same as above, this is a more sophisticated store with some higher prices. Talavera carries beautiful ceramics from all over Mexico including tiles from the Yucatan, masks from Guerrero, brightly painted wooden animals from Oaxaca, and carved chests from Guadalajara.

Unicornio
Av. 5 # 1

Unicornio specializes in Mexican folk art, including ceramic notions and etched wooden trays, but you'll have to sift through a lot of souvenir junk to find the good-quality items.

CHAPTER VII

DIVING MAGICAL, MYSTICAL COZUMEL

An Underwater Magic Show

DIVE COZUMEL

For many, the definition of Cozumel is diving. Ever since Jacques Cousteau discovered the diving on the reefs of Cozumel in 1961 divers have flocked to this Caribbean Island paradise. Because diving in Cozumel is drift diving (exactly what it sounds like), little energy is spent on swimming and bottom times are much longer. Visibility in the crystal blue waters is usually 100 ft or more, sometimes reaching 200 feet.

The marine life here is awesome, bright, and beautiful. Colorful fish and coral, huge lobster, crab and Manta Rays. Giant sea turtles, and if you are lucky, you may see some dolphins, sharks, and even some seahorses. Dive at night and it becomes a magical mystical world of sea life.

If you have never dove before, most dive operations offer the resort course, which will teach you basics and allow you your first dive. This gives you a chance to sample the sport and make a decision to continue or not. There are over 45 dive operations on the island, I strongly advise that before you choose one that you log on to one of the Cozumel or Scuba discussion boards and ask questions. Divers are quick to share their satisfaction or disappointments about their dive experiences.

I have listed what I believe is most or all of the dive operations on the island, and a description of most of the dive sites. If for any reason I have missed an operator, I apologize and it is not to reflect badly on that operator, just inquire about him on the discussion boards.

A note about shore diving. Shore diving is available on the island, not as great as the diving available by boat, but still fun and interesting. Tanks are available at $6–$8 U.S.. Dive the old plane wreck in front of the La Ceiba, it has some nice marine life, and makes a neat night dive.

HAPPY DIVING, AND PLEASE DO NOT TOUCH THE CORAL.

DIVE OPERATIONS

ALDORA DIVERS WWW.ALDORA.COM 011-52-987-872-4048
frontdesk@aldora.com 646-723-0667
Call or email for rates

AQUA SAFARI WWW.AQUASAFARI.COM 011-52-987-872-0101

2 Tank large boat	$60	additional dive $9
1 tank afternoon	$35	
2tank fast boat	$65	
Night dive	$40	
Snorkeler	$20	

Equipment rental and instruction available

ANITA DIVERS www.anitadiverscozumel.net 011-52-987-869-2683
Info@anitadiverscozumel.net 970-485-0909

2 tank $75

Contact for rates. Instruction and gear rental available.

AQUATIC SPORTS www.scubacozumel.com 011-52-987-872-0640

Scubacoz@scubacozumel.com

2 tanks $69
Email for other rates. Instruction and rentals available

BLACK SHARK   info@blackshark.com   011-52-987-872-5657

2 tank $55
Night dive $40
Cenote/cave $120

Equipment and instruction available.

BLUE ANGEL   www.blueangel-scuba.com   1-866-266-5639
                    blueangel@cozumel.com.mx

1 tank $45
2 tank $60
Night dive $40
Group and multi day available.   Instruction and rentals available.

BLUE BUBBLE   www.bluebubble.com   1-866-405-5749
                    Info@bluebubble.com

1 tank $40
2 tank $63
Night dive $63

Call for group and multi day packages.   Instruction and gear rental available.

BLUE NOTE   www.bluenote.com.mx   011-52-987-872-0312
                    COZUMEL@BLUENOTE.COM.MX

Email or call for rates.

BLUE XT SEA   www.bluextsea.com   011-52-987-872-3184
                    Info@bluextsea.com

2 tank $70

3 tank	$100	
Night dive	$45	Instruction available

Slightly higher than average, but Christi gets excellent reviews and divers return to her over and over. She is well known for going out of her way to help fellow divers, even when they are not her customers.

BUENA VENTURA   www.gocozumel.com/ventura 011-52-987-872-6014
                     Ventura@gocozumel.com

Contact for rates

CABALLITO DEL CARIBE www.seahorsecozumel.com 011-52-987-872-1449
                        Caballitocozumel@prodigy.net.mx

1 tank	$40
2 tank	$60
Night dive	$40

Multi day available   Instruction and gear rental available

CARIBBEAN DIVERS www.cozumeldiving.net/caribbean_divers
                                        011-52-987-872-1080

Call or email for rates   cdivers@prodigy.net.mx

CAREYCITOS ADVANCED DIVING www.advanceddivers.com
                                        011-52-987-872-0111
                                        Tony@advanceddivers.com

2 tank	$75

Contact for more pricing.   Gear and instruction available

CHINO'S SCUBA   www.xaac.com/chino   011-52-987-872-5836
                          Chino@coznet.finred.com.mx

Contact for rates.   Instruction and gear rental available

COSTA MAYA   www.iantd.com/coz/coz.html 011-52-987-872-4567
                          Dman@divecozumel.net   1-866-319-2649

Contact for rates.   Gear and Instruction available.

COZUMEL EQUALIZERS www.cozumelequalizers.com 011-52-987-878-4370
                          Info@cozumelequalizers.com   1-800-925-9939

Contact for rates.   Instruction and gear available.

COZUMEL SPORTS   www.cozumelsports.com   011-52-987-872-6726
                          sea turtle@prodigy.net.mx

2 tank $65
1tank $40
Night dive $40

Instruction and gear rental available.

DEEP BLUE   www.deepbluecozumel.com   011-52-987-872-5653
                          Scubadive@deepbluecozumel.com
Call for rates.

DEL MAR AQUATICS   www.delmaraquatics.net   011-52-987-872-5949
                          Reservations@delmaraquatics.net

Call for rates.   Instruction and gear rental available.

DIMI SCUBA   www.dimiscubatours.com   011-52-987-872-2915
                       Info@dimiscubatours.com

Contact for rates.   Instruction and gear rental available.

DIVE PALANCAR   www.divepalancarcozumel.com
                       moreinfo@divepalancarcozumel.com
                                                011-52-987-872-9770 x 8264

Contact for rates.   Instruction and gear rental available.

DIVE PARADISE   www.diveparadise.com   011-52-987-872-5161
                       Questions@diveparadise.com

1 tank $38
2 tank $55–58
Night dive $35

Instruction and gear rental available.

DIVE WITH MARTIN   www.cozumel-diving.net/martin
                              DWM@PRODIGY.NET.MX

1 TANK $45   011-52-987-872-2610
2 TANK $65
3 TANK $75

Contact for rates./multi day   Instruction and gear rental available
                                      free gear when available

DIVING ADVENTURES COZUMEL   www.divingadventures.net
                                   Sales@divingadventures.net
                                   011-52-987-872-3009

Contact for rates.   Instruction and gear rental available.

DRESSEL DIVERS   www.dresseldivers.com   not available
                       Sales@dresseldivers.com

Contact for rates.   Instruction and gear rental available.

EAGLE RAY   www.eagleraydivers.com   011-52-987-872-5735
                       Chellie@eagleraydivers.com

2 tank $65
3 tank $85
Night dive $45

Instruction and gear rental available.

ECO DIVERS   www.cozumel-diving.net/ecodivers
                       Ecodivers@cozume-diving.net

2 tank $60   1-800-849-7150

twilight 2tank $70
Night dive $45

Instruction and gear rental available.

EL GRAN AZUL   www.angelfire.com/ga/cozumeldiving/mmt.html
Victorbritto@prodigy.net.mx
011-52-987-872-3223

Contact for rates.   Instruction and gear rental available.

EMERALD DOLPHIN www.cozumel-diving.net/edds
Eddscozumel@prodigy.net.mx
011-52-987-872-3270

Contact for rates.   Instruction and gear rental available.

LUIS CABANAS   lusis@cozumel.com.mx   011-52-987-872-6745

Specialized in custom advanced dive trips, cave and cenote diving.
Contact for rates.   Instruction and gear rental available.

MANTA RAY   www.xaac.com/mantaray/index.html
Scuba@mantaray.com   011-52-987-872-6745

Contact for rates.   Instruction and gear rental available.

NITROX SOLUTIONS   www.islacozumel.net/diving/nitrox
NitroX@cozumel.czm.com.mx   1-800-967-1333

Contact for rates.   Instruction and gear rental available.

PAPPA HOGS   www.pappahogs.com   011-52-987-872-1651
Popshops@cozumel.net   1-877-389-3629

2 tank	$59
3 tank	$80
Night dive	$35

Instruction and gear rental available.

PEPE SCUBA www.cozumel-diving/pepe 011-52-987-872-6740
Pepe@cozumel.net home 6293

2 tank	$60
Night dive	$40

Contact for rates. Instruction and gear rental available.

ROBERTA'S DIVE ECO-COZUMEL www.robertasdiveecocozumel.com
Email on web site
011-52-987-872-4187/4240

2 tank	$65
2 tank twilight	$70
2 tank advanced	$70
Night dive	$45

Instruction and gear rental available.

SAND DOLLAR SPORTS www.sanddollarsports.net 1-866-737-6399
Infosds@sanddollarsports.net

Contact for rates. Instruction and gear rental available.

SCUBA DU DIVE www.scubadu.com 011-52-987-872-9505
INFO@SCUBADU.COM

Contact for rates. Instruction and gear rental available.

Scuba Tony WWW.SCUBATONY.COM 011-52-987-872-2248
Info@scubatony.com

Specialty is cave and cenote diving, but can arrange private open water trips.

SCUBA WITH ALLISON www.scubawithallison.com 011-52-987-989-6269
Allison@scubawithallison.com

A more personal approach to diving and instruction.

Contact for rates. Instruction and gear rental available.

SEA URCHIN DIVE www.seaurchindive.com 011-52-987-878-4888
Diving@seaurchindive.com

2 tank $64
2 tank twilight $65
Night dive $40

Contact for multi day rates. Instruction and gear rental available.

Formerly owned and operated by Isidro, many doubted Jorge would be able to carry on the high standards expected by Isidros customers. The reviews are in and Jorge has passed with flying colors.

WILDCAT DIVERS www.amproductions.com/wildcat.html
Wildcatcozumel@hotmail.com 011-52-987-872-1028

Contact for rates. Instruction and gear rental available

YUCATECH EXPEDITIONS www.yucatech.net not available
German@yucatech.net

For advanced divers who are interested in cave, cenote, and deep dives.

Contact for pricing and more information

COZUMEL DIVE SITES

Airplane Wreck(Shore) Skill Level: Novice
Location: In front of la Ceiba Hotel.
Conditions: Shallow and sheltered   Minimum depth: 33 ft/10 m
Maximum depth: 40 ft/12 m

This old DC3 40-passenger airliner was sunk deliberately in 1977 as a prop for a Mexican disaster movie, The hull was mostly all there until hurricane Roxanne hit in 1995 it is now broken up and scattered over the area, setting about 210ft/65m from the pier. The remains of the aircraft are now home to a large assortment of grunts and snapper. On the shore side of the wreck the sea bed rises rapidly to 17ft/5m and the numerous small coral heads have large numbers of Christmas tree worms and the split-crown feather duster on them. Hermit crabs, numerous shrimps and several species of blenny are among the sea fans and plumes.

Balones of Chankanaab
Depth: Shallow Dive: 60 to 70 feet
Skill level: Novice
A series of balloon—shaped coral heads. Lots of marine life, lobster and crab.

Barracuda Wall (Boat) Skill Level: Advanced
Location: South of Punta Molas Lighthouse, to the Northwest of the island.
Conditions: Strong currents expected; windy with Surface chop.
Minimum depth: 45 ft/14m
Maximum depth: beyond 100ft/30m

The most Northerly reef reached by any Cozumel dive operator, is seldom visited. Prior arrangements must be made through the harbor master. Due to the severity of the currents in the area, the number of divers per boat that can be carried on one trip is limited to six and all must be experienced open water drift divers, This is a flat strip reef with sand around, sloping into the depths. The attraction is the above-average chance to see large pelagic, such as barracuda, jacks, rays and sharks. Very large barrel sponges, rope sponges and elephant's ear sponge can all be found here.

Barracuda Reef (Boat) Skill Level: Advanced
Location: South of Punta Molas lighthouse, to the northwest of the island.
Conditions: A windy site with surface chop and strong currents.
Minimum depth: 69 ft/21 m
Maximum depth: Beyond 100ft/30 m

This site is visited but prior arrangements must be made through the harbor master. There are severe currents in this area, so the number of divers per boat is limited to six and all must be experienced open-water drift divers. This is a flat strip reef sand around, sloping into the depths. The attraction is the above-average chance to see large pelagic, such as barracuda, jacks, rays and sharks. The great barracuda (Sphyraena barracuda) is the most common species sighted. Diving here can be exhilarating, but hard work.

Barge Wreck (Shore, Boat) Skill Level: Intermediate
Location: Opposite the Vista Del Mar Hotel.
Conditions: Currents to be expected, windy and surface chop between November and April.
Minimum depth: 30 ft/9 m
Maximum depth: 40ft/12m

The barge was sunk in 1976 and is now abundant with sea life. There are many different corals and all sea life. The barge is 100ft., 30 m. long by 30 ft., 9m. Wide and 10ft., 3m. Height and sits upright on the bottom. There are two safe access points to the interior. The barge is a great night dive and photographers, should not miss it. There are large green moray eels and lots of black, Nassau.

Cedral Wall (Boat)
Depth: Deep Dive: 50 to 90 feet
Skill level: Intermediate

Expect a good ride on the usually strong currents. Kind of flat but full of color and marine life.

Chankanaab Caves (shore)
Depth: 35 feet max
Skill level: Novice

This is an interesting dive at the south end of Chankanaab Park. Excellent beach dive that can be reached either from Chankanaab Park itself or by entering south of the park towards Corona beach where there is no park entrance fee. Cold fresh water flows out of limestone caves called cenotes. Large Tarpan can be found swimming around in the entrance to the caves. Stay in the ambient light and do not venture far back. Interesting mixing of cold fresh water on the top layer with the warm salt water below.

Columbia Reef (Boat)
Depth: Deep Dive: 60 to 90 feet
Skill level: Intermediate
Impressive drop off at 60 to 80 feet. Deep diving at its finest, at least as spectacular as any part of the Palancar. A series of gigantic coral pinnacles, most over 90 feet, marked with caves, tunnels and caverns. Large marine life such as eagle rays, turtles and large barracuda often seen.

Columbia Shallow (Boat)
Depth: Shallow Dive: 15 to 35 feet max
Skill level: Novice
Maximum bottom time. This never ending sea garden is a favorite 2nd dive for maximum bottom time.

El Islote (Boat) Skill Level: Intermediate
Location: Close to Punta Celarain lighthouse traveling north toward the Maya ruins at Tumba del Caracol.
Conditions: An exposed location with unpredictable currents. This site is only accessible during the calmer months between may and September.
Minimum depth: 10 ft/3 m
Maximum depth: 30 ft/9 m

This single large coral Island is situated on flat sand and is a natural haven for all kinds of sea life. The shallower areas inshore split up into less distinct spur and groove reef formations. An interesting dive site, but there is always surge present. Good for parrotfish.

La Villa Blanca Drop-Off (Shore, Boat)
Location: Opposite La Villa Blanca Hotel.
Conditions: Strong currents to be expected, and surface can be choppy and windy.
Minimum depth: 69 ft/21 m
Maximum depth: Beyond 100 ft/30 m

This is a wall dive, but unlike the walls to the southwest of the island, which are vertical, it slopes steeply. This dive is one for experienced divers only. The currents can be quite strong and you do not get much chance to see the marine life unless it is swimming next you. If you dive from shore, make certain before you start that the current is running from the south to the north, this will make for an easier exit if you get swept away. A lot of work and questionable as to if it is worth the trouble.

La Ceiba Reef Preserve (Shore, Boat)
Location: Directly out from la Ceiba Hotel.
Conditions: Shallow, sheltered, good for beginners, photographers and snorkelers.
Minimum depth: 20 ft/6 m
Maximum depth: 40 ft/12 m
Skill Level: Novice

This is a ridge of coral and patch reef interspersed with sandy areas. There are star corals, brains corals, pillar corals and gorgonian sea fans. Beware of the Fire coral it HURTS. This dive is good for fish, sergeant majors and the yellowtail damselfish.

La Francesa Reef (Boat)
Location: Inner strip reef between Palancar and Santa Rosa reef.
Conditions: Moderate current and in most of this location, running from south to north.
Minimum depth: 40 ft/12 m
Maximum depth: Beyond 66 ft/20 m
Skill Level: Novice-Intermediate

This mostly unbroken strip and patch reef is the outer edge of la Francesa. It Bottoms out at 66 ft/20 m but the coral rubble and sand slope continues down to the outer reef edge and drop-off. The inside of the reef has a gradual slope of sand running down to the reef and, in some cases, sand chutes completely dissect the reef. Southern stingrays, peacock flounders and various mollusks are to be found on the sand. There are nice corals and a large supply of fish and invertebrates.

Little Caves (Boat)
Depth: Deep Dive: 50 to 70 feet
Skill level: Novice

Great dive with winding, colorful canyons, deep ravines and narrow crevices. Lots of passageways, tunnels and caves. Great dive at 50–70 f

Maracaibo Reef (Boat)
Location: Close to Punta Celarain lighthouse and south from Colombia reef.
Conditions: An exposed location with unpredictable currents. Only the most experienced of divers should consider diving this location.
Minimum depth: 60 ft/18 m
Maximum depth: Beyond 100 ft/33 m
Skill Level: ADVANCED ONLY

This very deep reef and steeply inclined wall are subject to unpredictable currents. When descending through open water to reach the descending terraces you must move swiftly and keep close in to the reef or you may be swept away from your planned position on the reef. You can look in wonder at the complexity of the old coral limestone structures, caverns, caves and swim throughs. Only the most advanced divers should dive here and only with supervision of an experienced local dive master carrying a signal marker buoy and a very experienced boat captain.

Palancar Caves (Boat)
Depth: Deep Dive: 60 to 90 feet
Skill level: Intermediate

Abundant marine life. Deep buttresses, tunnels, caves and big caverns. Very popular deep dive

Palancar Gardens (Boat)
Depth: Shallow: 40 to 70 feet
Skill level: Novice

Best dived from 40 to 50 feet. Beautiful dive with many large caverns.

Palancar Horseshoe (Boat)
Depth: Deep Dive: 25 to 125 feet
Skill level: Intermediate

A series if tightly pack giant coral heads rise from 100 feet to within 20 feet of the surface. One of Cozumel's busiest deep dives.

Paradise Reef (Boat, Shore with a long swim)
Depth: Shallow Dive: 40 to 50 feet
Skill level: Novice

A series of three separate reefs running parallel to shore approximately 200 yards out. This is the only reef accessible to beach divers. All three sections have abundant marine life including the reclusive Splendid Toad Fish, reputed to live only in Cozumel. Most popular spot for night dives.

Punta Tunich Drop-Off (Boat)
Location: Opposite Punta Tunich, several hundred yards or meters further out than Yucab, but running parallel with the reef.
Conditions: Generally strong current and choppy surface conditions.
Minimum depth: 50 ft/15 m
Maximum depth: Beyond 100 ft/30 m
Skill Level: Intermediate

The Northern end of this reef is the most interesting, but it is better to approach it when there is south-to-north current running. The wall at this end is near vertical, with numerous caves and crevices, which bisect the reef, running from the crest at around 66ft/, 20m down to much deeper water. Squirrelfish and pairs of angelfish can be approached fairly easily. A number of very large green moray eels can be seen along this reef.

Paso del Cedral Reef (Boat)
Location: Opposite to Punta Cedral to the inside of and running parallel to Santa Rosa reef.
Conditions: A moderate current runs from south to north. Can be windy on the dive boat.
Minimum depth: 33 ft/10 m
Maximum depth: 60 ft/18 m
Skill Level (novice)

Good photography dive with lots of opportunities to photograph schooling fish. There are large Schools of grunt and snapper, particularly the blue striped grunt and the schoolmaster. The Corals are fairly short, as you would imagine on this exposed strip reef, but where the reef is cut by sand chutes there are some very interesting small coral, such as disk coral and cactus coral. The southern stingray feeds in the sandy areas to the inside of the reef. Among the many mollusks is the occasional the queen conch, which is becoming scarce.

Paso del Cedral Wall (Boat)
Location: The next large reef system to the south and west of Paso del Cedral Reef.
Conditions: Unpredictable strong currents are to be expected. Minimum depth: 40 ft/12 m
Maximum depth: Beyond 100 ft/30 m
Skill Level: Intermediate

This site is similar to Santa Rosa Wall. It is less convoluted with fewer huge coral buttresses, but still very spectacular. Large grouper hang off the edge and numerous parrotfish are all over the area. Large encrusting and tube sponges, and several species of gorgonian fan corals are to be seen.

Palancar Shallows (Boat)
Location: About 2 km (1 mile) offshore, inside and parallel to the Planacar Drop-off and to the north.
Conditions: Slight-to-moderate current. Exposed on the surface.
Minimum depth: 17 ft/5 m
Maximum depth: 69 ft/21 m
Skill Level: Novice

Very interesting reef offering a wealth of diving experiences without the need to travel far. It rises to about 60 ft/18 m. The strip reef is more than 66 ft/20 m wide in much of the area and is cut and dissected by many fissures and caves. There may be current flowing over the reef, but there are so many sheltered areas and shallow water that it never causes problems Large stove-pipe sponges fan out from the reef and there are black coral in the deeper areas. Bright yellow tube sponges may be associated with juveniles of the yellow head wrasse and other fish hide in the deep tubes for protection at night. Butterfly fish, angelfish, parrot fish and damsel fish can always be seen. To the south, before Palancar Caves the reef drops much lower and becomes less defined. Do not miss this dive!

Palancar Garden (Boat)
Location: About 2 km (1 mile) offshore, inside and parallel to the Planacar Drop-off and to the north.
Conditions: Slight-to-moderate current. Exposed on the surface.
Minimum depth: 17 ft/5 m

Maximum depth: 69 ft/21 m
Skill Level Novice

See description for Palancar Shallows.

Palancar Horseshoe (Boat)
Location: South of Plancar shallows, but before Palancar Caves is reached.
Conditions: Windy and exposed on the surface, There can be strong current, but it is sheltered in the horseshoe.
Minimum depth: 30 ft/9 m
Maximum depth: Beyond 100 ft/30 m
Skill Level: Intermediate

This is a natural amphitheatre shaped like a giant horseshoe in a stretch in Palancar reef. There is plenty for any diver to enjoy in just one spot. The dive is best in the deeper section, which is deeply convoluted. Large gorgonian sea fans stretch out into the current and there is an array of fish, corals and invertebrates. The caves always attract divers, but you have to be very careful with controlling buoyancy so that you do not knock into the minute coral organisms that inhabit these shady areas. Remember to take a light with you to seethe true colors of the animals and corals

Palancar Caves (Boat)
Location: South of The Horseshoe.
Conditions: There is generally a current, but you will scarcely feel the effect of it until you emerge through the caves on to the outer wall of the reef.
Minimum depth: 20 ft/6 m
Maximum depth: Beyond 100 ft/30 m
Skill Level: Intermediate

Although this is classified as a deep dive, the shallowest part of the reef comes to within 20 ft/6 m of the surface. The reef slopes outward to the reef edge and deeply convoluted lip. Here, the corals seem to take on a life of their own as they form spires and buttresses, caves, gullies and canyons. Deep fissures run under the corals and sand slopes plummet into the depths. Large sheet corals jut out from the reef, creating interesting overhangs, which squirrel fish and bigeye seek during the day. There are countless caves and canyons along this stretch of reef and you will never be able to see all of them even after several dives. Schooling fish, such as grunts and snapper, constantly appear, and if you take your time as you exit the caves on the outer edge of the reef, you may glimpse a green turtle or a spotted eagle ray cruising past the wall

Palancar Deep (Boat)
Location: The outer of the reef wall south of the Horseshoe and Palancar caves.
Conditions: Exposed on the topside, and current is to be expected. Divers may experience difficulty climbing into the dive boat due to the sea swell.
Minimum depth: 40 ft/12 m
Maximum depth: Beyond 100 ft/30 m
Skill Level: Intermediate

This deeply incised wall is an absolute delight. There are so many different combinations of coral, you are never bored. Gorgonian sea fans on top of the reef and there is constant competition for space between the corals, sponges and algae. All are brightly colored and seem to have their own associated fish, crustaceans or invertebrates. Look out for a number of cleaning stations along this reef. Several different species host these locations, such as juvenile Spanish hogfish on the reef top, the cleaning goby among the coral head and the Pederson's cleaning shrimp among the tentacles of various species of anemone in the recesses.

Paso el Cedral (Oak Pass) (boat)
Depth: Shallow: 35 to 60 feet
Skill level: Intermediate

A series of many reefs marked with expansive low profile caverns at the beginning and lots of big fish. Less dived than most spots, but not to be missed.

Punta Sur Reef (Boat)
Location: South of Punta Sur at the southern entrance to laguna Colombia.
Conditions: This site can be very exposed during extreme weather conditions and there is always current. Minimum depth: 80 ft/24 m
Maximum depth: Beyond 130 ft/40 m
Skill Level: Advanced

There is an inner strip reef, which rapidly falls away to what is becoming one of the most popular dive locations on the island. Although the site can be visited only when weather permits, the sheer majesty of the deep wall, caves, caverns and fissures put the site at the top of most divers' lists. You enter the larger of the cave systems down a sand chute at 90ft/27 m where you enter a superb complex of coral tunnels and caverns, which are absolutely bursting with life. One of the larger caves, called the Devil's throat, opens up into an underwater room with four passageways, one of which leads to the Cathedral, a vast cavern with another three passageways, all interconnecting. The usual angelfish and butterfly fish can always be spotted swimming in pairs along the reef edge. The deeper coral walls have whip corals, which spiral out into the depths, and large black corals. There are also brightly colored small gorgonian sea fans, such as the deep-water fan, and sea whips, including the devil's sea whip, are very much evidence. This is an awesome dive, but bottom time is limited because of the extreme depth and the complex nature of the site.

San Francisco Reef (boat, Shore)
Depth: Shallow: 35 to 50 feet
Skill level: Intermediate

Begins on the Southern end of Old San Francisco Beach. This half mile reef is broken into three sections, separate by about 60 yards of sand. This is Cozumel's shallowest wall dives and loaded with life between 35 and 50 feet.

San Juan Two (Boat)
Location: South of Punta Molas lighthouse, to the Northwest of the island.
Conditions: Strong currents always expected; windy with surface chop.
Minimum depth: 52 ft/16 m
Maximum depth: Beyond 100ft/30 m
Skill level: Advanced

San Juan Two is a continuation of San Juan Reef. Severe currents flow through this area and the number of divers per boat is limited to six experienced open-water divers. This is a flat strip reef with sand around, sloping into the depths. This is the Northerly range of reef corals in this area of the Caribbean and the few varieties of coral that grow in this area are large. Large pelagic fish, such as eagle rays and sharks, are sometimes encountered around this site also.

San Juan Reef (Boat)
Location: South of Punta Molas lighthouse, on the same reef as San Juan Two.
Conditions: Strong currents always expected; and only for experienced divers.
Minimum depth: 69 ft/21 m
Maximum depth: 80 ft/25 m
Skill level: Advanced

Similar to San Juan Two, but the terrain is more uneven. Permission to dive must be granted by harbor master. Wire coral and purple sea fans are common, but the large pelagics are the attraction here; the gray reef shark (Carcharhinus perezi) is often seen. This dive is not for the faint-hearted. It is a long way to journey just for the chance of seeing big fish, and exploring it is hard work. There is a natural amphitheater called Pino's Bowl.

Santa Maria Reef (Boat)
Depth: Shallow: 40 to 60 feet
Skill level: Intermediate

This reef begins where San Francisco ends. A little less coral but large schools of angelfish.

Santa Rosa Wall (Boat)
Location: Next large reef system.
Conditions: Unpredictable strong currents are to be expected. There is always shelter however, when you reach the reef.
Minimum depth: 33 ft/10 m
Maximum depth: Beyond 100 ft/30 m
Skill Level: Intermediate

Easily be split into three separate dives. Its profile becomes larger and more convoluted the further North you travel. As in any exposed area, the Southernmost section is low-lying and scoured by currents. The middle section has some very large tunnels which completely cut through the reef crest, and the most northerly section has tunnels, caves, overhangs and under-hangs and some sections of wall becoming so steep they are near-vertical. On the steeper slopes there are numerous rope sponges. File clams can be seen in the recesses, their orange or white tentacles waving in the current. Many species of hermit crab can be found and there appear to be thousands of tiny gobies and blennies flitting in bursts over the corals and sponges. Barracuda and large specimens of the back grouper which shelter under the overhangs above the reef crest, can always be observed here. Stoplight parrot fish seem to blend into the multi-colored reef. Only when you use an underwater torch does true beauty of the reef reveal itself. One of the most distinctive of the small reef fish is the fairy basslet. The front half of its body is a brilliant violet-to-purple and its rear is a deep yellow/gold. These fish are instantly recognizable, but very hard to photograph because of their constant motion.

Torments Reef (Boat)
Location: South of Chankanaab Marine National Park and before Yucab reef, directly opposite Punta Tormentos.
Conditions: There can be very strong current.
Minimum depth: 30 ft/9 m
Maximum depth: 69 ft/21 m
Skill Level: Novice-Intermediate

An exposed, wide spread, broken-up patch reef system interspersed with wide, sandy channels.. It drops steeply to 69 ft/21m on the outward side of the slope, where there is a secondary reef. The reef consists of around 60 separate coral heads covered in a wide variety of brain corals, sea fans and whip corals. Colorful sponges in the canyons and there are many invertebrates hiding in the rocky crevices. At the end of the dive, as the current takes you gently north, there is a huge underwater formation similar to a terrestrial sand dune. Although the current can occasionally be strong, the boat captains are experienced along this reef and will drift along with you in the current. Schools of Creole wrasse move over the reef crest, and Bermuda chub and yellowtail snapper are well used to being fed.

Virgin Wall (Boat)
Depth: Deep: 40 to 130 feet
Skill level: Expert

Heavy currents prevent dive masters from bringing in large groups of inexperienced divers. 2 to 4 different dives to experience it all.

Yucab (Boat)
Location: To the South of PuntaTormentos.
Conditions: There is usually current. The reef is scoured by sand movement and has many archways and overhangs.
Minimum depth: 40 ft/12 m
Maximum depth: 69 ft/21 m
Skill Level: Novice-Intermediate

Although all these reefs are essentially drift dives, Yucab also offers shelter from the current on the outer edges, where underwater photographers can be inspired by every color in the rainbow. The sand-scoured overhangs also offer refuge for lobsters, banded coral shrimps and the arrow crab. There are also large numbers of squirrel fish and angel and butterfly fish always swimming in pairs. Lots parrot fish can be found around the live coral and you can hear their crunching on the coral..

Yucab Wall (Boat)
Location: Due west of Yucab.
Conditions: Current is to be expected, but the numerous large overhangs and tunnels across the reef offer plenty of protection for divers wanting to explore its recesses.
Minimum depth: 33 ft/10 m
Maximum depth: Beyond 100 ft/30 m
Skill level: all

This site is favored by a number of diving operations and it gets particularly busy along the outer reefs. Large coral buttresses jut out and form a convoluted, scalloped outer reef edge with numerous gullies and swim throughs. Like most of the outer reefs, Yucab Wall does not have many fish, but the fish that inhabit the site are large—such as black grouper. This is a particularly nice dive and its popularity is well deserved.

Marine Park Rules

Mexican government declare a National Marine park on July 19, 1996; covering area of more than 11 thousand hectares including the beaches and waters between Paradise Reef and Chiqueros point. The environmental, natural resource and fishing Secretariat SEMARNAP, administers the park.

The financing of the parks programs is shared by the federal government and the civil environmental groups; represented by COPRENAT, and the dive operators through ANOAAT.

Do your share to preserve the flora and fauna for future generations.

Corals are fragile.

Kicking, touching, dragging your gear causes damage, buoyancy control is your key to healthy coral.

Photographers in particular, take pictures without causing damage.

Marine organisms are protected by law.

Fishing, feeding the fauna and taking souvenirs is against the law. Refrain from extracting or annoying the marine flora and fauna.

Help us prevent pollution.

Report fuel, oil, sewage and garbage spills to the National Park office.

Pressure your dive operator to instruct novice divers and divers without adequate buoyancy control, and to refuse service to destructive divers.

If you use gloves, do not grab the corals.

If you carry a knife, keep it in the sheath.

Use biodegradable sun block products.

Local dive boats.

CHAPTER VIII

FISHING
FOR THE BIG ONE

FISHING IN COZUMEL

Well before Cozumel became a diving Mecca, it was considered to be one of the top world class fishing destinations for sports fishing. You can bottom fish, sports and deep sea fish, or fly fish, whatever your heart's desire, there is an operator in Cozumel to give you what you want.

Your choice of operators is diverse. You can go with the expensive top of the line fishing boats and pay top dollar, or you can go out with one of the less expensive operators, who has an older boat, but wonderful crews, and the equipment works the same, after all the fish don't know if that bait is hanging off a yacht or a row boat.

Depending on the season you can expect to catch Sailfish, Blue and White Marlin (these are catch and release only), Wahoo, Grouper, Snapper, Dorado (Dolphin, Mahi-Mahi) and Barracuda just to name a few.

The prime fishing season is March through October. Local fisherman fancy catching dorado (mahi-mahi), Wahoo, kingfish, sailfish, blue and white marlin and grouper (to name but a few). The crews supply the necessary fishing gear, lures, bait, beverages and snacks. You provide the energy.

During the high season (April through July) you can expect to catch Blue Marlin, White Marlin, Sailfish, Dolphin and Tuna. Year round, expect to catch Wahoo, Grouper, Barracuda, Mackerel, Amberjack and Snapper.

Sports fishing is primarily catch and release,. Pull that beauty in, take the picture and send him back to tease other fisherman. Grouper, snapper, Mahi Mahi, yummy, these guys are all keepers. Let the crew fillet them, share some with the crew and take the rest to your villa or a restaurant for cooking. Couldn't get it any fresher.

Tournaments

April

International Sport-fishing Tournament: This event brings together serious fishermen from all over the world to fish for mahi-mahi, tuna, blue marlin, white marlin, sailfish, Wahoo and red snapper. Each afternoon at 5pm the weighing begins. Be sure to be on the pier as each crew brings their catch to be qualified.

May

National Sport-fishing Tournament: This is an exciting weekend when all local and nationally registered boats compete for thousands of pesos in prizes including cars, boats, motorbikes and cash. You can catch the morning rally at the main ferry pier downtown where the beer is flowing and the water balloons are flying! Each afternoon at 5pm you can join the fishermen on the same pier to watch as each fish is weighed and scored.

CHARTER OPERATORS

3 HERMANOS   www.cozumelfishing.com   011-52-987-872-6417
                    Scathed@prodigy.net.mx   1-651-755-4897

ALBATROS CHARTERS   www.cozumel-fishing.net   011-52-987-872-7904
                        Info@cozumel-fishing.net   1-888-333-4643

½ day   1–6 people $400
¾ day   1–6 people $500
Full day 1–6 $550

MANETTO ADVENTURES   www.manetto.com   011-52-987-872-6695
                         Charter@manetto.com   1-817-429-1382

| ½ day | 1–6 people Aug–June $400 | Feb–July $500 |
| Full day | $500 | $550 |

MARATHON www.haciendasanmiguel.com/marathon.htm
Info@haciendasanmiguel.com

½ day	$450 Jan–May 14	$500 April 15–May 30
	June–Dec	
Full day	$500	$550

OCEAN TOURS www.cozumeldiving.net/oceantours 011-52-987-872-1379
ocean tours@usa.net

| ½ day | $440 |
| Full day | $549 |

SCUBA DU www.scubadu.com/Fishing/fishing.html 011-52-987-872-9505
Email on web site

| ½ day | $393 |
| Full day | $523 |

U. B. CHARTERS www.fishanddive.com 011-52-987-876-8538
Email on web site 1-704-795-0079

| ½ day | $350–450 |
| Full day | $500–600 |

WAHOO TOURS www.wahootours.com 044-987-8000304
Jim@wahootours.com

| Deep sea ½ day | $350 |
| Full day | $450 |

Bottom Fishing $300
    Full day $375

Individuals can request a share charter and Wahoo will attempt to arrange the share. $125 per person

Also can arrange private diving, including spear fishing, and snorkel tours.

Our family has used Wahoo for years, my boys love the crew.

My son and friends fish with Wahoo.

SPANISH FISH NAMES

AMBERJACK	PEJE FUERTE
BONEFISH	MACABI
BONITO	BONITO
DOLPHIN/MAHI MAHI	DORADO
GROUPER	MERO
JACK	JUREL

POMPANO	PALOMETA
RED SNAPPER	HUACHINANGO
SAILFISH	PEZ VELA
SHARK	TIBURON
SNAPPER	PARGO

CHAPTER IX

BEACHES–TOURS THINGS TO DO

You can't get bored here!

BEACHES, TOURS AND THINGS TO DO

If you don't dive or fish, not to worry my friend, there is so much else to do in Cozumel, you will not have time to get it all in. There are beaches to swim and snorkel at, or just relax, read a book, get a suntan, and let the waiters bring you a cold drink.

There is a wide assortment of tours and tour companies, sight seeing and other activities. Spend a morning exploring the ruins of San Gervasio, take a horseback ride on the beach or thru the jungle. Play a round of mini golf after dinner, or enjoy the real thing at the Cozumel Country Club.

If your stay is a week or longer, take a trip to the mainland to see the larger ruins and nature parks. I have not included mainland activities in this book, but any of the tour operators on the Isle will be able to help you with those. Remember, the most important thing, HAVE FUN!

A Cozumel Beach.

BEACHES AND BEACH CLUBS

SOUTH

Dzul Ha Beach Club: Probably the most popular and one of the best locations to snorkel from shore. This is a rocky shore, not sandy, but the snorkeling is so good, it is worth it. Be sure to wear beach shoes or booties, not only for the rocks, but the vast amount of sea urchins in the water. You can snorkel with out going to the club right next to it, but the club has a nice patio dining area and equipment rental.

PAL MAR Beach Club: Just slightly before Dzul Ha is a small club owned by Sherry Davis, with a nice large fresh water pool, sunning area, drinks and snacks, and equipment rental. Just walk across for the snorkeling.

Uva's Beach club: A small beach are with pool, snack bar, and pool. Never crowded, so a peaceful time for relaxing.

Chankanaab Park: A popular tourist attraction and often crowded. That said, it has a large sandy white beach for relaxing on. Good service on the beach for food and drinks, and excellent snorkeling. See Tour and activity section for further information.

Mr. Sancho's Beach: www.mrsanchos.com
One of my personal favorites, and my teen boys also. Has a beautiful white beach with a pool and Jacuzzi. Bar has neat swings for seats, but be careful after a few Margaritas. Restaurant serves pretty good food at the usual inflated beach club prices. Has a group of gift shops, and I have bargained for some good prices here. There are also Horseback riding and ATV tours available from here.

Nachi-CoCom Beach Club: A modern new beach club with beautiful restaurant, pool and Jacuzzi and beach. There is no admission, but there is a minimum $10 per person to be spent in food and drink.

Nachi Cocom

Playa Corona: You can snorkel here and see the same things as at Chankanaab, but without the crowds. You will be one of only a few on the beach. Has a seafood restaurant and gear rental.

Palm Beach: Not quite the same as Florida, but a very nice beach club. White beach, pool, and restaurant with candle light dinners served in the evening.

Playa San Francisco: Probably one of the most well known and nicest beaches on Cozumel. It is a 3 mile long beach, with access for divers to the San Francisco and Santa Rosa reefs. Besides the beach, there is a nice pool and also a children's pool, kayak rentals and a nice restaurant, whose prices are a bit high. Also has glass bottom tours available from here.

Paradise Beach: A large sandy beach, with an assortment of beach toys available. Kayaks, water trampoline, and water climbing rock have a $5 fee for use of all. Restaurant and drinks, with service on the beach.

Sunset in Paradise

Playa Mia Beach Club: www.playasol.com.mx
This club has a nice beach with plenty of beach chairs, a pool, entertainment, and a small Zoo. There is a $12 admission. A package can be purchased to include the buffet and an open bar.

Playa Palancar: The most southern beach, it is seldom crowded. Avery low key atmosphere to relax in. Has Restaurant, bar gear rental, and rest rooms.

Playa Caletita: Just slightly south of town, this is a small local beach area with snack bar.

Palapatita Beach Club: Another locals beach club, with small beach and bar. Good snorkeling. Close to Papa Hogs.

NORTH

Playa Azul Beach Club: A small beach club to the north of town. Has a $5 cover charge that is applied to your food and drink. Beach, pool, bar and restaurant.

EAST SIDE

Mezcallito's Beach Club: Located right at the end of the cross island road, this club can get a little wild at times, with tourists taking pictures next to the nude beach sign. Has a pretty beach for sunning, but remember swimming can be dangerous on the wild side. Good food and drinks.

Senor Iguana's Beach Club: Friendly little place, with nice beach, gift shop, Restaurant and drinks. Right next to Mezcalito's.

Punta Morena: Small beach club with good prices on seafood and drinks. Also has some basic rooms without electricity for rent.

Chen Rio Beach Club: A safe beach for swimming due to the rocks breaking the waves and current. Popular with locals especially on Sundays.

Playa Bonita: A long stretch of quiet deserted beach, safe to swim in the shallow water. Snack bar and drinks available.

Playa San Juan: A pretty nice beach area where it is safe to swim and wind surf.

TOURS AND OPERATORS

Atlantis Adventures: atlantiscoz@prodigy.net.mx   011-52-987-872-5671
If you would like to experience the Magical underwater wonderland of Cozumel, and you do not dive, well this one's for you. This is a real U S Coast Guard certified submarine. Go to depths of 100 ft and get an up-close viewing of the tropical sea life that Cozumel is famous for. Sub is air conditioned and small children are allowed. Cost is $70 adult and $45 for children 12 and under, or 36 inches tall.

ADVENTURE TOURS: www.travelnotes.cc/cozumel/tours/adventure.php

Offers an assortment of tours, some listed below.

Bike, go kart, snorkel tour: 4.2 miles of bike riding, 10 minutes of go karting, snorkeling and lunch at Dzul Ha. Includes all equipment, lunch and drink. approximately 3 hrs. $65 + $3 ins

ATV Wild Tour: ATV thru the jungle, kayak over Hanan barrier reef, snorkel. $94 single $79 double $52 child 6–11

Discover Scuba: Introduction to scuba, includes 1 dive. $55–$60

Dune Buggy Tour: Beach tour, Mayan ruins, snorkeling, picnic lunch.
Access isolated beach areas accessible by dune buggy or water only.
$89 adult $44.50 child 3–8

Jungle Horse Tour: Ride into the Mayan jungle, visit the oldest town on Cozumel at the el cedral ruins. 2 1/2 hours $30 +$3 ins age 8 or older only

Jungle Jeep Tour: Jungle and snorkel tour. Fascinating ruins, awesome snorkeling, Breakfast rolls, snacks, lunch and drinks. I have personally enjoyed this tour, it was great, especially for those who get to drive. 5 hrs $85

Jungle Trek: A hiking tour led by an experienced guide, includes swimming time. 3–4 hrs over 4 miles. $45 + $3 ins

Island Tour: A guided tour around the Island, includes ruins site, shopping, swimming, and a visit to wild east side. $75 4 hrs

Caballito del Caribe Pirate Ship   011-52-987-872-1449
Offers sunset cruises and Pirates night. Serves lobster dinner. Also Snorkeling tours.

Caribbean Bol: bowling@gocozumel.com
This is the brand new bowling alley on Ave 5 and Calle 13. Games are $45 mp and shoe rental is $15 mp. Modern electronic scoring and snack bar.

Chanankanaab Park: Besides the beach and snorkeling there are other activities her. Tour the beautiful gardens and view the replicas of Mayan artifacts. Swim with the dolphins.
Admission is $12, Dolphin activities are additional. The Dolphin swim is currently $120.

Cine Cozumel: Local modern movie theater located in the Chedraui shopping complex near Calle 11 and Melger. Movies are in English with Spanish sub titles, except for children's productions. Cost is way below what it is in the US, about $2.50 U.S..

Cozumel Country Club Golfing: 011-52-987-872-9579 Carreterra Costera Norte, 6.5 km
A fairly new 18 hole par 72 Championship course.
$149 including cart $99 after 1 pm

Cozumel Mini Golf: Calle 1 & Ave 15 www.geocites.com/smallsal/minigolf
Mini golf in the middle of tropical garden, complete with waterfalls and iguanas.
A challenging course, believe me I embarrassed myself. Order cervasa, sangria and
soda by walkie-talkie.
$7

Cozumel Sailing: www.cozumelsailing.com 011-52-987-869-2312/1777
Sailing and snorkel tours, barefoot sailboat rental, sunset sails. Owned and
operated by Capt. Dan and his First Mate Karen, you are sure to have a great time
with them no matter which activity you choose. A favorite of mine and others is
the Toucan tour, Includes a sailing trip, fishing, a grilled lunch, drinks, and
spinnaker rides, kind of Para—sailing in place. My bunch of teens had a blast.
Tucan $70 adults $40 children
Barefoot sailboat $100 first 2 hours then $25 per hour $12 per hr for crew or lessons
Sunset cruise $25 $18 no alcohol

spinnaker ride on the Tucan

El Cedral: The oldest Maya structure on Cozumel, built A.D. 800 is a very small
ruin, located at the very first town on Cozumel. Some small shops and a place for
snacks. Located a few miles up the southern beach road, free.

El Cementerio (The Cemetery)
At the south end of downtown's El Centro neighborhood, a 7 block walk from the downtown plaza, you'll find the old cemetery. Walk down the waterfront to the Post Office. Turn up Calle 7 and walk one block up to Avenida 5. Very interesting grave sites and mausoleums.

El Museo: A lovely museum with a lot of information about the history of Cozumel, located on the waterfront street, Melger between Calle 4 & 6. Tour the Museum and then have lunch on the balcony.
$5

Fury Catamarans   011-52-987-872-5145
Popular for it's snorkel, sail, and beach party tour, with lunch and all you can drink.
$60

Go Karts: 011-52-987-100-2429   cozumelgocarts@yahoo.com.mx
Located just south of Puerto Maya Pier. $10 for 10 minutes of racing around the track.

Mr. Sancho's Beach Club: Horseback riding and ATV tours, approx $30 per hour.

PARASAILING

Parasailing is provided along Cozumel's western shore, and boats can be flagged down from the hotel area south of San Miguel and at San Francisco Beach.

Punta Sur Ecological Park: An ecological park designed for educating visitors. Nesting turtles program, ruins, lagoons, and the Punta Celerain Lighthouse. Located on the southern tip of the island. Cost is $10 for the Museum and lighthouse.

Rancho Buenavista: 011-52-987-872-1537
Saddle up and enjoy guided tour on horseback thru the jungle and visits to several Mayan ruins.

San Gervasio Ruins: On cross island road approximately 7 km outside of the city. Not as big as the mainland sites, but still very interesting. This is where the Mayan women came from the mainland to worship.
$5

A resident iguana at San Gervasio

Sunday In the Plaza: A good time for all, and it is free. Music and dancing, as children play. This is a wonderful evening of people watching. Stroll around and enjoy the snacks offered by vendors. Bring candy and hand it out to the children. Not to be missed if you are in town on a Sunday evening.

Smiling faces

TEQUILA HISTORY TOUR: Along the cross island road that leads to it's Eastern Shore you will pass the Tequila Hacienda, where you can partake in a Tequila History Tour if you so desire. Each tour includes the opportunity to taste several types of tequila. $18 and worth it.

COZUMEL NIGHT LIFE

Although it isn't a party town when compared to Cancun or even Playa del Carmen, there is some night life to be found. The clubs tend to stay open until the wee hours of the morning, so if you plan on party time, then take a day off from diving the next day.

Carlos and Charlie's: 11 Melger Ave   011-52-987-872-0191
The same wild party that goes on in every port this chain is located. Loud music, Tex-Mex food, and plenty of dancing.

Hard Rock Cafe: 2A Melger Ave   011-52-987-872-5271
The smallest Hard Rock in the world, it makes up for it in Ear shattering music. Loads of fun for the younger crowd.

Havana Club: Melgar between Calles 6 and 8, 2nd fl   011-52-987-872-1268
For great jazz, good company, drinks, and great cigars, check out the Havana Club.

Neptuno's: Melger & Calle 11   011-52-987-872-1537
Catering to the Young crowd with techno music and laser shows.

SENOR FROGS 11 Melger Ave

Another version of Carlos and Charlie's, and located above them. Just hop on the escalator and ride on up.

Tony Rome's: Ave 5 between Salas and Calle 3
Now this is my speed. Excellent entertainment by Tony himself. This man can sing about anything you request. Dance on the large raised dance floor, or take the microphone and try some karaoke yourself. This is not an all night party, but it is lots of fun.

Viva Mexico: Av. Rafael E. Melgar   872-0799
A dance club that has a DJ who spins Latin and American dance music until the wee hours. Gets loud and crowded, but lots of fun. No connection to the Viva Mexico restraint..

CHAPTER X

MONEY-MEDICAL CHURCH & SPECIALTY SERVICES

Everything you may need on vacation.

MEDICAL, BANKING, CHURCHES, AND SPECIAL SERVICES

MEDICAL

The Medical care available in Cozumel is very good. There are hospitals, clinics, and Doctors who speak English and can provide excellent care. In the event of a catastrophic emergency you can be air evacuated to the US. I became severely ill with pneumonia and received outstanding care at the CMC clinic/hospital. I know others who have spent several days of their vacation in this hospital and received the same level of care.

Also available are Dentists, (people often save their dental work for here as the work is excellent and the prices low), a Chiropractor, hyperbaric chambers, and opticians. Please be aware that you will be expected to pay cash or credit card at most places and file with your insurance at home.

HOSPITALS AND CLINICS

CMC (Centro Medico de Cozumel) located on Calle 1. It's open 24 hrs., English speaking doctors, very modern, laboratory, air ambulance, associated with Miami hospital, air-evac, professional and friendly service. Phones 987/872-5664, 987/872-3370, 987/872-3545

Clinica San Miguel
Clinic offering emergency care
Small three bed clinic offering 24-hour emergency care. Specializes in pediatrics. Emergency room with modern equipment available and there are some English-speaking doctors.   Calle 6, 133 (between Avenues 5 & 10)   9872-0103

Clinica San Miguel: 872-0130
Clinica CEM: 872-2919
Clinica Medica del Sur: 872-5787
Social Security Hospital: 872-0140
IMSS: 872-0222
Clinica Villanueva: 872-0395
Clinica Guadalupe: 872-2508

Quiropractico de Cozumel: Avenida 5 between Calle 3 and 5: 872-5099
There is an excellent chiropractor, Dr. Scott Kircher. He speaks English fluently
and is knowledgeable in Spanish. He practices some unique "holistic" healing
that amaze those in pain. He won't pop your bones if you don't want him to, but
he will still help you.

Camera Hyperbaric: 872-1430
This is Cozumel's hyper baric chamber used mainly for diving accidents but has
been known to help stroke victims as well. The hospital has X-ray machines and
more. Dr. Pascual Piccolo is the resident doctor. They work well with Americans
and are fluent in both languages.

DOCTORS

DR. RECHY	872-2182
DR. JESUS MATEOS	872-5787
DR. JORGE ALVAREZ	872-2534
DR. LEWIS	872-1616
DR. PICCOLO	872-3070
DR.SERGOVIA	872-3545
DR. MORALES	044-987-876-0666 CELL
DR. PADILLA	044-987-878-5161 CELL

DENTISTS

Dr. Arteta   044-987-100-1576
Calle 17 & Ave 25

Speaks fluent English, all areas of dentistry including oral surgery.

Dr. Hernandez	872-0656
Dr. Mariles	872-1352
Dr. Luis Angel	872-0808

PHARMACIES

There are pharmacies on every corner in Cozumel. Many of our RX in the USA do not require a prescription here, except for the controlled drugs, such as narcotics. The pharmacist expects you to know what you need, and will loan you his PDA drug guide. Your best bet is to either look up the Spanish name before leaving home, or go to the American pharmacy where they can tell you the correct name. A short list of pharmacies is listed here, but that does not mean the others are not OK.

American Discount Drugstore
Medication at Bargain Prices English Spoken
Tel: (9) 872-4855

Los colores de Dori
2 North between Rafael E. Melgar & 5th Avenue
872-2238

El Kiosco
5th Street at 1st south
872-2485

Dori
5th Avenue at 7 south
872-5519

Paris
6th North between 5th and 10th North
872-3552

Portal del parque
5th Avenue South in between Juárez Avenue & 1st South
869-2119

Pharmacia Joaquin
5th & Plaza del sol Avenue
872-0195

La Placita
Juárez Avenue between 5th & 10th
872-5132

Portales
11th Avenue between Rafael E. Melgar & 5th Avenue
872-0936

Portales
10th Avenue #101 between Juárez
872-1048

Yza
5th Avenue between Juárez & 2nd North #50
872-2777

OPTICIANS AND EYE GLASSES

Dra. Concepción Planas Fernández
Calle 6 between Melgar and 5 Avenida, south side of the street
872-3805

She has a totally computerized system and does a thorough eye exam herself as well.

OptiCon
Avenida 10 between Calle 7 and Calle 9

Has a fair selection of frames at reasonable prices.

ENGLISH AA MEETINGS   6 pm daily   872-3836
Calle 5 & Ave 10

MONEY AND BANKING

There are a number of banks in Cozumel where you can exchange currency. Your resort or hotel may also offer exchange services, but their rates may not be as good. Convenience sometimes costs a bit more. There are also money exchanges and ATMs as well.

Serfin
10th Avenue #198 at the corner of 3rd Street
872-2853
Bital
5th Avenue at the corner of 1st Street
872-0142
Banamex
5th Avenue at 1st South & A. R. Salas
872-3411
Bancomer
5th Avenue at Plaza del Sol
872-0550
Banorte
5th Avenue at Juárez & 2nd North
872-0718

ATM MACHINES

You can find an ATM on every corner in the main town square. Keep in mind that the machines deliver pesos not U>S dollars. There is only one place to go if you need to make an advance on your credit card and want US$...BANAMEX downtown just inside the main town square when entering from 5th Avenue and Adolfo Rosada Salis.
My advice is to use only the machines that are located attached to a bank, during banking hours. That way if there is a problem you can resolve it immediately. These are only a few of the locations available.

PROMOCION Y OPERACION, S.A. DE C.V.
1A. AV. SUR #11

. PROMOCION Y OPERACION, S.A. DE C.V.
CALLE 1A. SUR NO. 13 POR 5A.

. BANCO MERCANTIL DEL NORTE S.A.-INSTIT.DEBANCA MULTIPLE,
GRUPO FINANCIERO BANORTE
AV. 1A. SUR ENTRE CALLE 5 Y 10

CITIBANK
ADOLFO ROSADO
ADOLFO ROSADO
COZUMEL, 77600

BANCO MERCANTIL DEL NORTE S.A.-INSTIT.DEBANCA MULTIPLE,
GRUPO FINANCIERO BANORTE
AV. PEDRO JOAQUIN CODWELL

BANCO INTERNACIONAL CA
AV. RAFAEL E. MELGAR
ENTRE 3 Y 5

LAS PALMERAS RESTAURANT

BANORTE-Cozumel
AV RAFAEL MELGAR # 27—A

Cozumel Money Exchanges

Like a bank, money exchanges can convert your current currency at the going rate in pesos. You may get a slightly better rate from one to the next, or even at one of the banks. Check around. It is a good idea to be familiar with the exchange rate before you go!

These places are located all over Cozumel, but I list a few to get you started.

Asesores turísticos y cambiarios
5th Avenue # 121
872-0276

Consultaría internacional
1 st South & Plaza Confetti
872-4480

Diamond exchange
R. E. Melgar # 111
872-2043

Monex Av. Juárez $
10th Avenue
872-4222

CHURCH SERVICES

CATHOLIC CHURCHES
Parroquia San Miguel 10th Avenue at Avenida Juárez

Corpus Christi 20th Avenue between 15 and 17th St.

Iglesia de Guadalupe 65th Avenue at 8th Street North

PRESBYTERIAN SERVICES

Templo Evangelico Presbiteriano Juarez Avenue between 40 & 45th St.

Nueva Iglesia Presbiteriana 11th Avenue at 90th Street

Ebenezer Presbyterian
Ave Pedro Joaquin Coldwell between 8 and 10 ENGLISH SERVICES ON
SUNDAY AT 9AM
872-3400

GREEK ORTHODOX
EBEN EZER P.J. Coldwell between 8 and 10th Street North.

Non-Denominational Christian   In English
Calle 11 between Ave 15 & 20

Jehovah Witness 2 locations

Ave 65 between Calle 7 & 9

Calle Rosado Salis

Church of Jesus Christ
Ave 40 and Calle 4
872-4167

Church of Latter Day Saints
Calle 4 and about 45 AV

INTERNET AND CALLING STATIONS

Do <u>NOT</u> use the red phones that you see everywhere on the island. These are
<u>VERY, VERY</u> expensive and you will regret it!
There are calling stations and Internet cafes all over the city, and in the
neighborhoods. Here are a few to help if you can't seem to find them.

Diamond Internet Café
Ave 10 #200 between Calle 4 & 6
9am–9pm Mon-Sat

THE CALLING STATION
Ave Rafael Melgar at Calle 3
Long distance phone calls and fax service.
Open 7 days a week.

The Coffee Net
Melger & Calle 11, just across from Acuario
You can check your e-mail (through Netscape, AOL, and Hot Mail, among others

Internet and Calling Station
Ave 5 between Salas & Calle 3
This is where I usually go. They are very friendly and have some of the best prices in town.

LAUNDRY SERVICE OR SELF SERVICE

Laundry prices usually run $10 to $15 pesos per kilo.

Lavanderia Mañana—Calle 11 in Plaza Los Arcos Drop off and pick up.

Lavanderia Margarita—872-2865
Avenida 20 between Adolfo Rosado Salas and Calle 3. Drop off and pick up.

Lavanderia Express—872-2932
Adolfo Rosado Salas between Calle 5 & Calle 10. Coin operated.

Tintoreria Del Mar—872-5470
Avenida 20 between Adolfo Rosado Salas & Calle 1. Reliable dry cleaning.

Lavanderia Rosita—872-1262
Calle 40 X Hidalgo—Drop off and pick up.

Lavanderia Industrial Joaquin—872-1648
Industrial laundry

MASSAGE AND SPA SERVICES

AQUA SPA   011-52-987-872-1421
Ave 10 & Calle 10

Offers massage, wraps, facials, manicures, and pedicures.

Barefoot in Cozumel   www.barefoorincozumel.com   011-52-987-878-4662

Owned and operated by Sally Hurwitch, I can vouch personally for her skills, ahhh feels so good. A practioner of Swedish massage, Reiki, and Ashiatsu Bar Therapy for 9 years, she practices in the quiet peaceful surroundings of her island cottage. Rates start @ $45 per hour.

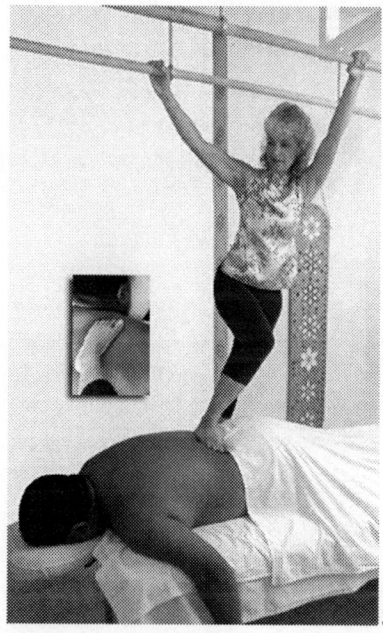
Sally of Barefoot in Cozumel

CARRIBEAN MASSAGE   011-52-987-872-5068
Ave 5 #313 between Calle 3 & 5

Offering massage, aromatherapy, and hairdressing.

COZUMEL MASSAGE   WWW.MEMBERS.AOL.COM/CZMMASSAGE
Helen@cozumelmassage.com

Owned and operated by Helen Green who was trained in London England. Several different arts of massage, and also offers hair and makeup services.

SUE'S WELLNESS CORNER   www.cozumelmassage-wellnesscorner.com
@ El Cid La Ceiba   suescorner@hotmail.com
                             872-0844

Massage, reflexology, injury treatment, Jacuzzi sauna and showers

BEAUTY SALONS: You can expect to pay anywhere from $4.00 to $10.00 for a cut at most island shops. Manicures are priced around $6.00 and up

Kenny Villanueva—La Estetica
Av. Juarez and 55th Ave
Cuts, foils, highlights, color, pedicure, manicure, body massage
English Spoken

Don Cabello
Corner of Ave 20 and 25TH Street
Cuts, color, manicure
Limited English Spoken

Island Creations
Ave 50 between 14th and 16th Streets
Cuts, color, eyebrow wax
By appointment Tele: 872-6284
English Spoken

Barney's
Ave 7 between 18th and 20th Streets San Miguel II
Cuts, color, manicure, pedicure at economical prices.

FLORISTS

Floreria Evelyn   872-4028
65 AV between Calles 16 & 18

Floreria Mariela   872-7686
1st Street between 15 & 20 Avenues.

WEDDING PLANNERS

COZUMEL WEDDING PLANNER   www.cozumelweddingplanner.com
                                Info@cozumelweddingplanner.com
                                011-52-987-872-4878

Make your special day a stress free one. Leave the planning to Stephanie, who has been planning Cozumel weddings for many years.

SOMETHING SPECIAL   www.cozumelmexico.net/wedding-services
                          Info@cozumelmexico.net
                          011-52-987-872-5857

Fiona Anne Lomax will plan your wedding from a simple basic ceremony to a wedding spectacular.

ROMANTIC WEDDING DESTINATIONS
                          www.romanticweddingdestinations.com
1-866-412-2999   Cozumel@romanticweddingdestinations.com

Total wedding planning, from boarding your plane to starting the honeymoon.

VIDEO RENTALS

BLOCK BUSTER
Juarez & Ave 30

Offers most movies in English, except children's productions. Just sign up for free and it works the same as in the U.S.

CALLING STATION
Melger waterfront

Offers a small assortment of English movies and video players for rent.

CAMERA AND FILM SERVICES

ISLAND PHOTO AND VIDEO CENTER

www.islacozumel.net/services/armando

At the entrance to La Ceiba Hotel   011-52-987-872-5833

FULL SERVICE PHOTO LAB
CUSTOM VIDEO PRODUCTIONS
School of Underwater Photography & Videography
UNDERWATER CAMERA AND VIDEO SYSTEM RENTALS

Foto Omega
Melger & Calle 3

Offers developing and printing in minutes for 35MM, APS, or Digital Media

FujiFilm/ColorMax
Ave Juarez between 25 and 30 (across from the gas station)

Popular with locals and offers more reasonable prices than Omega, Fuji is a full-service operation offering cameras, film, supplies, and b/w film developing. 1–2 hour film developing available. This is where I have gone for 9 years, and am always satisfied.

Gyms

Muscle & Fitness Gym
Ave 55 between 5 and Hidalgo
Monday–Friday 6:30AM to 11:00PM, Saturdays 7:00 AM–9:00PM, Sundays 9:00AM–1:00PM

Muscle and Fitness is clean, cool and spacious, with a friendly staff. The monthly fee for using the gym facilities is 200 pesos. For an additional 50 pesos you can also participate in their aerobics classes.

Power Gym
located off of Ave 30 close to Calle 2 or 4.

CHAPTER XI

COMMUNNITY SERVICE

Open your heart and become a part of
Cozumel.

PEOPLE HELPING PEOPLE—COZUMEL COMMUNITY SERVICES

Those of us who are frequent visitors to Cozumel are very aware of all the organizations that serve the local population, which includes the Mexicans and those who have moved there from other countries.

In the USA there are government funds and corporate fundraisers who help to finance charities. That option is usually not available in Mexico. There is so much that visitors can do to help, sometimes without spending a dime, maybe just an hour of your time. Please read this chapter and keep all of those listed in mind. From the bottom of my heart, I THANK YOU.

AMERICAN COMMUNITY SERVICES/ACS   www.cozumelinsider.com/acs

ACS is a non-profit service to benefit the residents of Cozumel. They have 2 primary objectives.

1. To benefit the community by promoting and facilitating volunteerism and philanthropist activities.

2. To enhance the knowledge and experience of Americans in Cozumel by providing information and referral services for vacations, relocations. And working and living in Cozumel.

PROJECTS SPONSORED BY ACS

BLOOD DONOR DRIVE: In conjunction with the community blood bank they are working in 3 areas to benefit all of Cozumel.

   1. To establish viable donor registry comprised of both Amer4ican and Mexican residents that can be accessed 24/7 in emergencies.

   2. Identify a pool of potential donors who will be available when the blood bank has a specific need.

3. Work with the medical community to launch a campaign to educate the local residents about the need for donors, and to dispel the myths about donating blood.

COZUMEL CLEAN PROJECT

This is a trash pickup project comprising a group of the local children. They work together to clean up and keep clean their neighborhoods. ACS volunteers coordinate the children's efforts. If you are on the Isle when one of these days are scheduled, come out and help. Supplies are always needed: trash bags, surgical gloves, cotton gloves. All can be dropped off at the ACS office located at 602B Melger, next to the Navy base.

CARNAVAL FUND RAISING FOR THE CHILDREN

Funds are collected to assist with the cost of the children's participation in dance groups during Cozumel. If it were not for this assistance many children would be unable to participate in their local Carnaval traditions.

Contact Sherri Davis @ 011529878690504 for further information. You might ask her if you can donate costumes as well, like those used in your children's and grand children's recitals.

MARINE TURTLE SALVATION PROJECT

A partnership with the Municipio de Cozumel to save the sea turtles from extinction. For hundreds of years turtle meat was a staple of the Mayan diet. The younger generations must be educated and strong efforts made to protect these turtles before they are gone forever. Currently there are 2 programs in operation.

1. The Parks and Museum Foundation's Punta Sur Park Salvation program is a for profit program which offers tickets @ $40 for excursion to view the turtles.

2. The City of San Miguel's volunteer salvation program covers the beaches from Mezcilito's to Punta Sur Park entrance. The city depends on volunteers, police, and the armed forces assistance on the east side of the island, during nesting season. Volunteers do most of the nightly work. Cash contributions are not usually accepted, but contributions of supplies are always welcome and sorely needed.
Low level flashlights, infrared lights, batteries, 2 way radios, latex gloves, pens, water proof markers, and gas vouchers are always needed. Read more about these projects and the effect the recent hurricane Emily has had @ www.cozumelinsider.com/turtles

CASA HOGAR PARA NINOS

This is an orphanage located in Cuidad del Carmen where a large group of children ages 3–18 are cared for. In years past there has been a yearly Christmas gift collection, both funds and gifts were accepted.
Please contact Lisa@Caldwell web.com

CHRYSALIS

http://geocities.com/smallsal/chrysalis/   cozkids@hotmail.com

Chrysalis is solely dedicated to helping the children of Cozumel who are in need, to achieve their full potentials.
This special program owns a large part of my heart and a percentage of any proceeds from this travel guide will be donated to Chrysalis to assist in furthering the education of these children.

Education in Mexico is not free, nor is it inexpensive for the needier families in Cozumel. Many children are deprived an education, as their families are unable to afford the costs associated with sending them to school. Registration fees, required uniforms, textbooks and school supplies can amount to one or two months of a family's total income.

The Cozumel Chrysalis Group assists financially those children who show a desire for education but are unable to attend due to the expense involved.

Chrysalis began in 1995 by a small group of expatriate ladies who wanted to "DO SOMETHING". In the first year 10 students were assisted to attend school, in 2005 there are over 250 who are able to attend school due to the efforts of this group.

This group is pure Non-profit, absolutely NO ONE is in a paid position. Every one that gives of themselves and their time, does so for free and for the love and appreciation of these children. I myself am a volunteer, although not able to do as much as I would like, as I do not live on the Island. I give my time at Carnaval working the booth, assist with shopping for those supplies, and dedicate most of my luggage each trip to bringing clothing for the yard sales, Carnaval beads, and school supplies. Also a part of what you paid for this book will be given to this organization.

HOW TO HELP!

Sponsorship: A one time donation of $80 U.S. for elementary students, or $200 U.S. for a Jr/Sr high schooler will provide for 1 full year of a child's education. If you are unable to donate this much, consider a small cash/check, even $5 will help.

Used clothing sale: Bring good/clean used clothing in your luggage each trip. These are sold at yard sales and helps families two ways. They are able to buy good clothing for a few pesos, and then those pesos add up and are used for purchasing uniforms and supplies. Supplies and clothing can be dropped off at Cozumel Mini Golf, Alicia's B&B, or just call 1-866-511-1014 and arrange for pick up.

School supplies: Check the web site for current needs, but usually pens, markers, book bags, calculators are on the list. Check first for specifics.

Carnaval Booth: This project is the # 1 fundraiser for Chrysalis. A booth is set up during Carnaval and beads, masks, and other carnaval trinkets are sold. Donate your throw beads from Mardi Gras, purchase a few novelty beads and bring them, the same with masks. Offer to carry some of our purchased supplies over on your trip. If you will be here during Carnaval, offer to work a shift at the booth. You will make new friends, helping the children, and have a load of fun.

Whatever you do, do something. Every little bit helps. Look at your own children and grand children and think how terrible it would be if they were unable to get any education. THANK YOU.

CORAL PARK BUDDY PROGRAM

A fund raising program to save the reefs of Cozumel. Make a donation at www.coralreefalliance.org/divein/parkbuddy
Or go to the site to read about the projects underway to protect and save the reefs. Contact is Eileen Weckerle @ eweckerle@coral.org or 1-888-coral-reef.

DIVE WITH MARTIN DONATIONS: Accepts used prescription glasses and hearing aides. He will reward you with a free dive for 2 pairs of glasses or 1 hearing aide. Email DWM@prodigy.net.mx

HUMANE SOCIETY OF COZUMEL

www.islecozumel.net/services/spca
011-52-987-857-0849

Founded in 1996 with a one-time grant from the government, they are now only able to continue operation with the donations and volunteer services of those who care.

SERVICES:

At cost Vet services.
Spay-neuter program.
Adoption program
Free euthanasia

There are several ways you can help this worthy organization.

1. Volunteer a few hours or a few days of your trip. Help clean up, work on repairs, or just walk and play with the animals.

2. Adopt a dog or cat to take home. The shelter will assist with arrangements.

3. Donate supplies. Always needed is medical supplies, surgical gloves, and bandages, call and ask.

4. Cash donations ALWAYS welcome.

CHAPTER XII

LET'S SPEAK SPANISH

Basic Spanish for vacation.

You could manage quite well in Cozumel with out ever speaking a word of Spanish, but please remember we are the guests. Most of the people who work in the tourist industry there can speak some English and understand pretty well. But if you at least make an attempt to speak in their language, you will not be laughed at, but receive a big smile and maybe some help with your Spanish. If you venture into some of the less tourist areas, you will find you are able to do so much more just with the basic words and phrases, so come on give it a try.

Tip: Use sticky notes and label everything at home in Spanish, without the English, you will quickly pick up words that way.

Basic Interactions

Hola
hi

adiós
goodbye

sí
yes

no
no

por favor
please

gracias
thanks

muchas gracias
thanks a lot

dispénseme
excuse me

perdón
pardon

OK
OK

de nada
you're welcome

hasta mañana
see you tomorrow

hasta luego
see you later

adelante
come in

siéntese
sit down

repita
say it again

traduzca
translate

señor
sir

señora
madam

señorita
miss

el amigo
the friend (male)

la amiga
the friend (female)

el esposo
the husband

la esposa
the wife

salud
cheers, gesundheit

PHRASES

¿Cómo se llama usted?
What's your name?

Me llamo (María).
My name is (Maria).

Mucho gusto.
Pleased to meet you.

¿De dónde es usted?
Where are you from?

Soy de (Nueva York).
I'm from (New York).

¿Habla inglés?
Do you speak English?

Hablo un poco de español.
I speak a little Spanish.

¿Cómo se dice…en español?
How do you say…in Spanish?

¿Qué significa…?
What does…mean?

¿Cómo se pronuncia esta palabra?
How do you pronounce this word?

el teléfono público
the public telephone

los servicios
public toilets (1)

los baños públicos
public toilets (2)

el paradero de autobuses
the bus stop

la estación del metro
the subway station

el estacionamiento
the parking garage

el museo
the museum

el semáforo
the traffic light

la farmacia
the drugstore

el mercado
the market

el poste de luz
the streetlight

la calle
the street

la policía
the police

el cruce
the intersection

el letrero
the street sign

la panadería
the bakery

la esquina
the corner

el basurero
the trash basket

el/la peatón(a)
the pedestrian

la librería
the bookstore

el taxi
the taxi cab

la avenida
the avenue

el zócalo
the main square

el quiosco de periódicos
the news stand

el supermercado
the supermarket

PHRASES

¿Dónde están los servicios higiénicos?
Where is the bathroom?

¿Dónde están los baños públicos?
Where is the bathroom?

¿Dónde está el paradero de autobuses?
Where is the bus stop?

¿Puede ayudarme?
Can you help me?

No comprendo.
I don't understand.

Me he perdido.
I'm lost.

¿Dónde está la zona comercial?
Where is the main area for shopping?

¿Hay una guía telefónica?
Is there a phone directory?

¡Socorro!
Help!

Mi dirección es…
My address is…

Hotel Spanish

el cuarto de baño

the bathroom

la cama
the bed

la pensión
the boarding house

el cuarto doble
the double room

el ascensor
the elevator

la llave
the key

la entrada
the lobby

el/la gerente
the manager

servicio de cuarto
room service

la ducha
the shower

el portero
the porter

el botones
the bellhop

el huésped
the guest

el balcón
the balcony

con aire acondicionado
air-conditioned

la bañera
the bathtub

la cuenta
the bill

el recibo
the receipt

el desayuno
the breakfast

la cena
the dinner

el almuerzo
the lunch

cuarto con desayuno
bed and breakfast

la cama matrimonial
the double bed

pensión completa
full board

media pensión
half board

PHRASES

¿Puede recomendarme un hotel barato?
Can you recommend a cheap hotel?

¿Cuánto cobra por noche?
What's the cost per nite?

¿Hay algo más barato?
Is there anything cheaper?

¿Tiene cuartos libres?
Do you have any vacancies?

Quisiera un cuarto sencillo.
I'd like a single room.

¿Me permite ver el cuarto?
May I see the room?

No hay agua caliente.
There isn't any hot water.

No me gusta esta habitación.
I don't like this room.

¿Cuánto cuesta por semana?
What's the weekly rate?

¿Están las comidas incluidas?
Are meals included?

Dining Out

la bebida
the beverage

bien cocido
well-done

la cuchara
the spoon

el cuchillo
the knife

la cuenta
the bill

la mesa
the table

el mesero/el camarero
the waiter

el menú
the menu

menú del día
set menu

el pan
bread

picante
spicy

la pimienta
the pepper

el pimentero
the pepper shaker

el platillo
the saucer

el plato
the plate

poco cocido
rare

el postre
dessert

la propina
the tip

la sal
the salt

el salero
the salt shaker

la servilleta
the napkin

la tarjeta de crédito
the credit card

la taza
the cup

el tenedor
the fork

el vaso
the glass

PHRASES

¿Qué está incluido?
What is included?

¿Viene con ensalada?
Does it come with salad?

¿Cuál es la sopa del día?
What is the soup of the day?

¿Qué me recomienda?
What do you recommend?

¿Puede darme...?
Can you bring me...?

La cuenta, por favor.
The bill, please.

Estuvo delicioso.
That was delicious.

¿Dónde hay un buen restaurante?
Where is there a good restaurant?

Quisiera reservar una mesa para dos.
I'd like to reserve a table for two.

¿Qué clase de...tiene?
What type of...do you have?

Shopping

el carrito
the shopping cart

la cesta
the basket

la carnicería
the butcher's shop

la panadería
the bakery

el quiosco
the newsstand

la tienda de modas
the clothes shop

la papelería
the stationery shop

la plaza del mercado
the marketplace

la zapatería
the shoe shop

caro(a)
expensive

barato(a)
cheap

ir de compras
to go shopping

comprar
to buy

pagar
to pay

abierto
open

cerrado
closed

cerrado al mediodía
closed for lunch

la tarjeta de crédito
the credit card

la joyería
the jewelers

la salida
the exit

la entrada
the entrance

de mejor calidad
better quality

el recibo
the receipt

defectuoso(a)
defective

roto(a)
broken

PHRASES

¿Cuánto cuesta?
How much does it cost?

Es demasiado caro.
It's too expensive.

¿Tiene algo más barato?
Do you have anything cheaper?

¿Puedo probármelo?
Can I try it on?

El color no me sienta bien.
The color doesn't suit me.

¿Dónde están los probadores?
Where are the changing rooms?

Voy a pagar al contado.
I'm going to pay cash.

¿Puede atenderme?
Can you help me?

Sólo estoy mirando.
I'm just looking.

¿Podría mostrarme…?
Could you show me…?

Medical

la medicina
the medicine

la cápsula
the capsule

la tableta
the tablet

la píldora
the pill

la inyección
the injection

el ungüento
the ointment

descanso en cama
bed rest

la cirugía
the surgery

la toalla calentadora
the heating pad

la bolsa de hielo
the ice pack

el soporte
the sling

el enyesado
the cast

la muleta
the crutch

el médico
the doctor

la enfermera
the nurse

el salpullido
the rash

los escalofríos
the chills

el dolor
the pain

alta presión sanguínea
high blood pressure

el resfriado
the cold

la torcedura
the sprain

la infección
the infection

la fractura
the broken bone

la cortada
the cut

el golpe
the bruise

PHRASES

Estoy enfermo(a).
I'm sick.

¿Dónde le duele?
Where does it hurt?

¿Tiene fiebre?
Do you have a fever?

¿Desde cuándo se siente así?
How long have you felt this way?

¿Podría llamar a un médico, por favor?
Could you please call a doctor?

¿Puede visitarme el médico?
Can the doctor come here?

Tengo náuseas
I feel nauseous.

Tengo alergia.
I have an allergy.

Tengo diarrea.
I have diarrhea

Tengo migraña.
I have a migraine.

Beach time

la playa
the beach

el mar
the sea

tomar el sol
to sunbathe

la piscina
the swimming pool

el/la salvavidas
the lifeguard

el colchón neumático
the air mattress

la sombrilla
the umbrella

la pelota de playa
the beach ball

los lentes oscuros
the sunglasses

el traje de baño
the bathing suit

la ola
the wave

nadar
to swim

la arena
the sand

el respirador
the snorkel

la crema solar
the sunblock

la concha marina
the sea shell

la nevera
the cooler

el/la bañista
the sunbather

el agua
the water

el planeador de mar
the surfboard

el planeador pequeño de agua
the kickboard

la costa
the coast

la toalla
the towel

la marea alta
the high tide

la marea baja
the low tide

PHRASES

¿Hay algún salvavidas?
Is there a lifeguard?

¿Es seguro para niños?
Is it safe for children?

¿Es seguro nadar aquí?
Is it safe to swim here?

¿Podemos nadar aquí?
Can we swim here?

¿La playa es de arena?
Is the beach sandy?

¿Se puede bucear aquí sin peligro?
Can one dive here without danger?

¿Hay una contracorriente peligrosa?
Is there a dangerous undertow?

¿A qué hora es la marea alta?
What time is high tide?

¿A qué hora es la marea baja?
What time is low tide?

¿Hay una corriente fuerte?
Is there a strong current?

Airport talk

la maleta
the suitcase

el equipaje
the baggage

el boleto
the ticket

el guardia de seguridad
the security guard

el detector de metales
the metal detector

el seleccionador de rayos
the x-ray machine

la banda
the conveyor belt

el carrito de equipaje
the baggage cart

el maletero
the porter

la sección de no fumar
the non-smoking section

el pasaporte
the passport

el talón
the baggage claim ticket

el maletín
the carry-on bag

la aduana
the customs office

el reclamo de equipaje
the baggage claim area

el pase de abordar
the boarding pass

el, la sobrecargo
the flight attendant

el compartimiento de equipaje
the luggage compartment

la mesita
the tray table

el pasillo
the aisle

la terminal
the terminal building

la pista
the runway

el vuelo
the flight

el ala
the wing

la cola
the tail

PHRASES

¿Qué terminal necesita Ud.?
What terminal do you need?

Busco la terminal norte.
I'm looking for the north terminal.

¿Para dónde sale Ud.?
Where are you headed?

Voy a México.
I'm going to Mexico.

La terminal norte es para los vuelos internacionales.
The north terminal is for international flights.

¿Dónde puedo reclamar mi equipaje?
Where can I claim my luggage?

¿Dónde está la aduana?
Where is customs?

Por favor, ¿me puede ayudar con las maletas?
Could you please help me with my bags?

¿Me permite ver su talón?
Could I see your baggage claim ticket?

¿Cuántas maletas tiene?
How many bags do you have?

Days & Months

January	Enero
February	Febrero
March	Marzo
April	Abril
May	Mayo
June	Junio
July	Julio
August	Agosto
September	Septiembre
October	Octubre
November	Noviembre
December	Diciembre
Monday	Lunes
Tuesday	Martes
Wednesday	Miércoles
Thursday	Jueves
Friday	Viernes
Saturday	Sábado
Sunday	Domingo

Colors

White	blanco
Blue	azul
Red	rojo
green	verde
yellow	amarillo
Black	negro

Numbers

Zero	cero
One	uno
Two	dos

Three	tres
four	cuatro
five	cinco
six	seis
seven	siete
eight	ocho
nine	nueve
ten	diez
eleven	once
twelve	doce
thirteen	trece
fourteen	catorce
fifteen	quince
sixteen	dieciséis
seventeen	diecisiete
eighteen	dieciocho
nineteen	diecinueve
twenty	veinte
thirty	treinta
forty	cuarenta
fifty	cincuenta
sixty	sesenta
seventy	setenta
eighty	ochenta
ninety	noventa
one hundred	cien
one thousand	mil

CHAPTER XIII

USEFUL INTERNET SITES

Discussion board sites and lots of useful information.

DISCUSSION BOARDS AND HELPFUL INTERNET SITES

The discussion boards listed are ones that I use every day, as do many other frequent visitors and Cozumel locals. These boards are the best place to get your questions answered. Everyone is friendly, and they will welcome you with open arms. I have met many of my friends on these boards and even better have met many of them in Cozumel. We often arrange parties at one of the local restaurants, where everyone who is on the Isle at the same time gets together, including many of the locals. So come on, join in and make some Cozumel friends.

DISCUSSION BOARDS

BOOTS N ALL TRAVEL www.bootsnall.com/insiders/namerica/mexico.shtrr

List of insiders from all of Mexico, willing to answer any question you might have about their area.

COZUMEL MY COZUMEL www.cozumelmycozumel.com

Owned and moderated by Carey Sutton an American expatriate living in Cozumel for several years now, and previously a long time visitor. She offers great forums and information, articles on living and visiting on Cozumel. Also has a list of villas for rent, and monthly Cozumel news translated into English.

COZ GUIDE. NET www.cozguide.net

Online travel guide for Cozumel and Riveria Maya. Includes a chat room and an abundance of information.

COZUMEL INSIDER   www.cozumelinsider.com

Not a discussion board, but offers a wealth of information for visitors and locals alike.

COZUMEL UNDERGROUND http://wahootours.hyperboards2.com/index.cgi?

Forum sponsored by Jim Wilson of Wahoo Tours. Jim's daily posts of news and Cozumel happenings are fantastic and often entertaining. Frequented by Cozumel locals and frequent visitors to the Isle, you can definitely get your questions answered here.

MY COZUMEL COMMUNITY www.cozumel-hotels.net/yabbse/index.php

Yet another great forum with information related to Cozumel and more. Moderated by Tony Rome, a twenty year resident of the Island. Have a problem on Cozumel CALL TONY!

TRAVEL NOTES COZUMEL www.travelnotes.cc

Forum where you can ask question or just visit with Cozumel locals and visitors. Links to tours, hotels, dining, and lots of reviews.

SCUBA BOARD   www.scubaboard.com

Has a forum specific to diving in Cozumel. Great place to inquire about dive operators etc.

THE GRINGO GUIDE   www.gringoguide.com

Cozumel forum and trip reports.

OTHER USEFUL SITES

OFFICIAL COZUMEL SITE   http://www.islacozumel.com.mx/homeing.asp

Official government welcome to Cozumel.

Cozumel Click   http://www.cozumel-click.com/homepage.html

Offers a great deal on a discount card for dining and tours, even on villa rental. I have used the card, and it is well worth it.

Cozumel-Cancun Travel
http://home.pcisys.net/~ronlee/Scuba/Cozumel/Aug2001/CancunCozumel.htm

Great in depth information on the Riveria Bus for travel between Cancun and Cozumel.

Cedral Homes   http://www.cedral.net/

Builder's site with information about building a home on Cozumel.

Playa del Carmen Transportation
                            http://www.entertainment-plus.net/tour_tpt_pdc.cfm

Van transportation between Cancun Airport and Playa del Carmen.

Cancun Travel   http://www.cancuntravel.com/transfers.asp

More van options from Cancun

Seat Guru. Com   http://www.seatguru.com

Cool site for picking the best seats on air craft and avoiding the bad.

Metric Conversions   http://www.sciencemadesimple.net/conversions.html

Great site for converting those metric measures into something familiar to us Americans.

ATM Locator   http://visa.via.infonow.net/locator/global/jsp/SearchPage.jsp

Locate ATMs anywhere in the world.

Map Chick   http://www.mapchick.com

Offers a great mini guide to Cozumel on a map. You will be surprised how much is on there. A must have.

Currency Converter   http://www.xe.com/ucc

Offers up to date currency conversion. Put the amount in and convert.

Translation Service   http://www.freetranslation.com

Offers free translation online.

Trip Advisor   http://www.tripadvisor.com

Find reviews on Hotels and more.

LAST MINUTE TIPS BEFORE YOU GO!

#1 TIP: "Travel with an open mind; be thrilled, not provoked, with things that are different." Harvey S. Olson, chairman of Olson-Travelworld Organization

If you do not like hard beds bring a mattress pad or foam pad with you. Most beds in Cozumel are on platforms of some kind and they are extremely firm.

Toilet paper is not always available in rest rooms, bring tissues and wet wipes to keep on you.

Bring scented candles or air freshener. At some times of the year rooms have a very musty smell, due to the humidity?

Don't forget the bug spray, also try some bounce softener sheets tucked into your blouse or shirt, the mosquitoes do not like it and stay away.

Make copies of your passport, Birth certificate, and important papers to keep in your wallet. Lock up the real stuff.

Drop off your laundry for washing the day before you leave the Island, and go home with clean cloths.

Bring large resealable plastic bags for those last minute wet bathing suits and wet suits.

The Electricity in Mexico is 110 Volt, 60 cycles, like the USA. It may be a problem to find the modern three prong outlets in some places, so you may need a two/three prong adapter.

Tap water should be considered unsafe. Bottled water and purification tablets or drops are cheap and readily available. Restaurants only use purified water, so they are safe. Get in the habit of not using tap water to rinse your mouth when brushing teeth; close your mouth in the shower

You can take the sting out of that sunburn by dabbing or spraying on white distilled vinegar after a cool shower. It really works! You may smell like a lovely tossed salad for a while, but a small price to pay for relief.

Always keep some loose change or small bills in your pocket—you never know when you're going to need some for a tip.

If you do not speak Spanish, bring a small notebook or calculator for writing prices when negotiating.

Consider bringing Pepto Bismal. I have heard that taking Pepto Bismal twice or four times a day keeps most people from getting Montezuma's Revenge.

Keep essentials, such as a change of clothing, in your carry-on bag. Lost luggage is a fact of travel life and locating lost bags takes an average of three days. I know about this, I once wore the same outfit 3 nights in a row.

Purchase a Club Caribe Card for great discounts in dining and tours. http://www.cozumel-click.com/homepage.html

A few things that are nice to bring with you are a fold up cooler, insulated drinking cup, cork screw and bottle opener, extra film and batteries

You can buy lottery tickets in Cozumel. It's fun and could extend your vacation if you are lucky. I buy mine at the Mercado at the newspaper stand.

978-0-595-36995-9
0-595-36995-2

Lightning Source UK Ltd.
Milton Keynes UK
23 March 2011

169681UK00001B/203/A